I0825513

Praise for *Puddle Jumpers*

"Brandon Webb has cracked the code: Real resilience isn't built by pushing kids harder, but by giving them the space and support to trust themselves, discover what lights them up, and grow through challenge. *Puddle Jumpers* is the practical guide for building the kind of inner confidence that helps kids withstand whatever pressures come their way—from school, from peers, from a culture that tells them they're never enough."

—Jennifer Breheny Wallace, author of *New York Times* bestseller *Never Enough*

"*Puddle Jumpers* is the rare parenting book that doesn't preach—it equips."

—Kristina Partsinevelos, CNBC Nasdaq correspondent and mom

"Years ago, I told Brandon to write a book about parenting. I wanted to see lessons from such a fantastic parent shared with the world. What he shares here will not only make you a better parent but a better version of yourself."

—Kamal Ravikant, author of *Love Yourself Like Your Life Depends on It*

"Part SEAL toughness, part entrepreneurial ingenuity, and all wrapped in fatherly love—*Puddle Jumpers* offers a fresh approach to parenting. It's about raising kids who embrace challenges, grow resilient through adversity, and discover the confidence to chart their own path."

—Dr. Chloe Carmichael, PhD, licensed clinical psychologist and *USA Today* bestselling author

"*Puddle Jumpers* is a powerful reminder that resilience is not innate but taught, day by day, in the small moments that shape a life. Brandon Webb brings the precision of an elite operator and the honesty of a devoted father to the hard, necessary work of raising capable, grounded kids in a chaotic world."

—Elliot Ackerman, *New York Times* bestselling author,
Marine veteran, and recipient of the Silver Star,
the Bronze Star for Valor, and the Purple Heart

"Former Navy SEAL Brandon Webb does it again! Only this time, instead of lessons on how to survive the dangerous war zones of Afghanistan and Iraq, he guides the reader through the most important 'Special Op' of all . . . successfully parenting (and co-parenting) children in a world with perhaps more land mines than in an actual war. And, in typical Webb style, he communicates his message with grace, humor, and solid how-to wisdom that will help today's parents raise their offspring to be ready and equipped to live their best and most successful lives possible! This book is truly a gift that will benefit generations to come."

—Bob Burg, coauthor (with John David Mann)
of the international bestseller *The Go-Giver*

"Brandon Webb has a rare gift for turning life's toughest lessons into wisdom we can all use. His new book isn't just a story; it's a masterclass in resilience, leadership, and living with purpose. If you want to learn what it takes to thrive when the stakes are high, this is the book to read."

—Jairek Robbins, performance coach
and bestselling author

Puddle Jumpers

MORE FROM BRANDON WEBB'S
LEADERSHIP LIBRARY:

The Red Circle
The Making of a Navy SEAL
Among Heroes
Total Focus
Mastering Fear

Puddle Jumpers

Powerful Mental Techniques from a Navy SEAL Performance Coach and Father of Three

Brandon Webb

Authors Equity
1123 Broadway, Suite 1008
New York, New York 10010

Cover design by Pete Garceau
Jacket Photograph © Getty Images / Evgeny Atamanenko
Book design by Scribe Inc.

Most Authors Equity books are available at a discount when purchased in quantity for sales promotions or corporate use. Special editions, which include personalized covers, excerpts, and corporate imprints, can be created when purchased in large quantities. For more information, please email info@authorsequity.com.

Library of Congress Control Number: 2025949096
Print ISBN 9798893311884
Ebook ISBN 9798893311808

Printed in the United States of America
First printing

www.authorsequity.com

To every parent out there, single, married, divorced, co-parent, foster, adoptive, step, or simply someone who stepped up when no one else did. This one's for you.

Puddle Jumper

noun | [*pud'l jum'pər*]

Definition: Brave, joy-seeking souls, especially children, who leap into life's messy, muddy moments with full-hearted abandon.

They see a half-frozen mud puddle and run for it, not from it. They're not scared of getting dirty, falling down, or looking like a lunatic while chasing what lights them up.

They live fully, laugh loudly, and don't flinch at a little chaos. They remind the rest of us—especially those adults hardened by the years, careers, and endless to-do lists—that true happiness isn't found in the clean, controlled parts of life. It's found mid-jump, covered in mud, grinning like a little maniac.

That's a puddle jumper.

And I'd take a team full of them any day.

Contents

Foreword

As we stood there watching the second tower fall on TV, Brandon looked at me and said, "I have to go."

I was shocked, yet I knew in my heart exactly what he meant. This was what he, and all of the SEAL Teams, had been training for. Not even twenty-four hours later, we had named our soon-to-be-born son, and Brandon was off to war. I was seven months pregnant with our first child, unsure of when I would ever see my husband again.

Life tends to test you in ways you could never imagine—tests that push you to your breaking point but also free you when you rise stronger from them. Parenting—and co-parenting—tests you in similar ways. It takes patience, communication, and above all, respect. Brandon and I have a deep appreciation for each other as co-parents.

This book comes from a place of wanting to help other parents be their best, no matter their circumstances. It's honest, practical, and rooted in lived experience, not theory. If you are a parent, I hope you take what you find here to heart. And if you are a divorced co-parent, I hope it reminds you how vital it is to lift each other up along this lifelong journey we call parenting.

—Gretchen Maybee

Introduction

We'd just come off the mountain after a great, long day on the slopes, legs smoked, everyone ready to chill out. While slogging through the parking lot back to my car, gear dangling off every limb, the youngest of my three kids, Tyler, spots it: a half-frozen puddle of slush and mud, so gnarly it looked as if it had its own ecosystem. I can still picture his face lighting up as he started running straight for it with the delight of a dog chasing a tennis ball.

Tired, cold, and looking forward to getting home in front of the fireplace, my default parent mode kicked in, ready to shut it down. I opened my mouth to snap, "Don't even think about it, T-Man!" But I suddenly stopped myself.

Why? Because in that split second, I realized something. By stopping him, I wasn't protecting him. I wasn't helping him. I wasn't really looking out for him at all. I was projecting my own adult hang-ups—the inevitable mess, the inconvenience of a drenched six-year-old on the drive home, the extra laundry, him looking ridiculous. Instead, I had to ask myself an important question all parents must ask themselves at times: *Why the hell not?*

So as he looked over his shoulder, I took a deep breath, smiled, and said, "Get after it, dude!" He launched in full send mode. Whooouush! Muddy ice slush all over his clothes and face, laughing like the little maniac he still is today. And that's when it hit me: These are the kind of kids I want to raise. Those who jump into life, not around it. I want to raise puddle jumpers, kids who aren't afraid to get dirty in pursuit of a joyful life.

As parents, we've got to check ourselves. Too often, we're shutting down our kids, not just out of our unfounded concerns or personal bias, but because we're dragging around our own baggage: fear of judgment, need for control, leftover perfectionism from childhood.

That day, I almost stomped out my kid's curiosity. But I caught myself. I let him jump into the mud, and boy am I glad I did, because this wasn't just about letting a kid be a kid—it was about clearing the runway to land. I've had some incredible jobs in my life, from Navy SEAL to entrepreneur, but being a dad tops them all. It's the one role that humbles you, teaches you, and pays you back in moments like this—muddy boots, wide smiles, and a reminder that you're the luckiest guy on earth.

Clearing the Runway

At twenty-eight, I became the head instructor of the US Navy SEAL sniper course. But over the next few years, even as I achieved the peak of my SEAL career, teaching the next generation of elite snipers, I started to feel the cost of that life. My marriage was on the rocks, and I could see the distance growing between me and my kids. After living on adrenaline during thirteen years of go-go-go deployments, followed by demanding ninety-hour work weeks as a sniper instructor, I had to face a hard truth: If I wanted any kind of future with my children, I needed to make a change. So I made the most difficult call of my life—I left the Teams. I chose my family over the Navy, knowing that no mission, no matter how critical, was more important than being there for my kids.

What I never expected was that the same mental management techniques I'd learned and used to teach deadly SEAL snipers would also apply to my transition to civilian life, along with all the land mines I'd encounter on the way: the loss of my first business, my entire life savings destroyed, divorce, and all the time spent trying to be a good father to my three children.

The core principles of being a great sniper align with those of any effective mental management program for performance, such as with sports: visualization (or mental rehearsal), a positive outlook in all situations, self-image management, and positive verbal cues. (The big difference, of course, is that missing a shot in, say, basketball is not a life-or-death situation.) As a dad, I've used these principles, along with my background as a former helicopter crewman and later pilot, to develop my own style of parenting. This proved to be an incredible tool and parenting hack for me as a divorced father of three.

My children are all different in their own ways. The oldest, Jackson, has always been interested in computers, math, debate club, music, and chess. He's more calculated and thoughtful in his decisions. Madison is in the middle, the creative one of the family and brave in everything she does. Tyler is the youngest; he's also great at math, though not very interested in academics, and sportier than his siblings. Like his dad, he wants to act without overthinking and contemplating every detail.

We are not a perfect family, and I'm not a perfect father. I've made plenty of mistakes, but regardless of my missteps, I can say I've been consistent with my love and support. And though we've been through a lot of tough times as a family, we've come out the other side better for it.

I deployed to Afghanistan right after the September 11, 2001, terrorist attacks as a Navy SEAL with Team 3 ECHO platoon. My wife at the time, Gretchen, was seven months pregnant with Jackson, and everything felt clouded in uncertainty. I later went to Iraq as a defense contractor, which was no cakewalk either. After losing my first start-up in 2008, my wife and I divorced, and a cascade of events followed: moving cities, and schools, multiple times; leaving friends behind; losing people my children were close to at a young age, particularly my friends in the SEALs; dealing with issues around drugs and alcohol; and handling the other typical challenges we all contend with as parents. Of course, those challenges are growing: On top of death, drugs, alcohol, sex, and family drama, we now have social media, the internet, and artificial intelligence changing the fabric of our society, not to mention our existence.

We've also entered a new era as parents. All of the tightrope-walking, shark-dodging, and dream-protecting we do for our kids often takes place without the village our grandparents took for granted. According to Pew Research, fewer than 30 percent of US parents live near most or all of their extended family, and many report feeling isolated in their parenting role. Further, academic findings show that modern parenting support is becoming increasingly individualized, meaning fewer hands in the fight, less shared wisdom, and more solo struggle.

The extended family used to live down the street—now they're a time zone away on FaceTime. Neighborhoods once raised kids shoulder-to-shoulder; now, most of us are winging it behind closed doors in big cities or isolated suburbs, searching for answers on the internet at midnight and hoping we don't screw up the one job that matters more than any other. That gap, the space where wise uncles, tough aunties, and watchful neighbors used to stand, needs to be filled.

There is little in the way of practical tools and advice (from actual parents, not academia) on how to raise kids in today's crazy world. Like most, I didn't take any parenting classes; I just started winging it. But I had an unfair advantage: my SEAL sniper training.

No Greater Mission

I'm not here to hand you an encyclopedic manual of parenthood. Hell, nobody could do that. What I am doing is laying down the parts that count, the lessons that left scars and the ones that saved my ass: a guide to parenting with intention, so you're not just reacting to fears, but shaping your child's future with purpose. This isn't theory; it's blood, sweat, and the kind of trial by fire that only raising kids can deliver. I'm filling the foxhole with every lesson I learned the hard way: self-taught, parent-tested, and refined through raising my own three kids with my co-parent and ex.

My hope is simple: that somewhere in these pages you find a tool, a phrase, or a mindset you can carry into your own battles at home. From one parent to another, I'm giving you what I've learned in the arena, because while we can't cover everything, we can damn sure focus on what matters most.

In recent years, as my kids grew into young adults and started college, I found myself being asked for parenting advice. The questions came from my circle of friends, new parents, and peers from business school and alumni communities, often after they'd spent time with my kids and walked away genuinely impressed by how they carried themselves. I'd even get asked for advice at conferences where I was the keynote. People were curious—especially when I told them my parenting system was based on techniques I developed as a Navy SEAL—and would always dig deeper, asking more questions.

So I finally decided to write this book and share my experience as a father. I'm not a parenting academic. Through most of my kids' early lives, I was a divorced dad. But as my kids developed into capable young adults, it became clear that their mom and I had done something right. I felt like I had something to offer other parents on their journey, sharing my own messy parenting experience and all the lessons I've learned along the way.

There's no greater mission as a parent than raising a child who knows who they are and has the tools to thrive and become the captain of their own life. It's an amazing feeling when your kids grow up and blossom into happy adults, and you realize they are truly prepared to handle the world on their terms. And that's the real goal: You must prepare your children for the world, not protect them from it.

I still remember my daughter Madison visiting me in 2024 during her summer break from Goldsmiths, University of London, where she was a design student. Over dinner at my favorite French restaurant, Grenache, in Lisbon, she told me, "Dad, I just want you to know I am exactly where I want to be in my life, and I appreciate you allowing me to be myself."

What an amazing thing to hear as a parent.

It's these moments that powerfully reveal the return on our investment for all those years of being a consistent parent who shows up every day.

By guiding our children to become happy adults, we're not just shaping their future either—we're contributing to a stronger, more compassionate humanity. I think we can all agree that, considering the state of the world, this is a good thing.

What I'm going to teach you forever changed my life for the better. The principles in this book have helped me greatly, and if you commit to them, they will remain with you for years to come. You'll be a better parent, grandparent, spouse or partner, and person for it.

If you're thinking, "My kids are too old, and I've missed the boat!" I want to stress that "No, you haven't." It's never too late to learn these lessons in mental management. I didn't learn them until I was close to thirty years old. These techniques have also helped me deal with my own father-son dynamic with my dad, Grandpa Jack to my kids.

Having kids is not easy, especially in the ultraconnected world we live in today, where negativity is just a click away, but there's hope!

At the core of this book, my primary mission is to equip you for the rewarding yet demanding journey of parenthood. I want to help you raise kids who are not just happy by their definition but also kind, curious, and independent doers. Or as I like to describe them, puddle jumpers.

The Only Easy Day Was Yesterday

Just as I'm not a perfect father, nobody is a perfect parent; we all struggle with the hands life deals us. However, the imperfections, mistakes, and stressors, when handled correctly as parents, make our children blossom into beautiful adults. In most cases, it's all necessary. We went through hell as a family, and my kids still turned out to be joyful, bold, and resilient.

In the SEAL Teams, we have many sayings, but the one that most applies to being a parent is the same creed I still live by: "The only easy day was yesterday." As parents, we must bring our best effort every day, even on our bad days, which we all have. I've seen too many SEALs get comfortable, even cocky, and then get sent back to the regular Navy for not bringing their all to the job daily. Yesterday's challenges are gone, in the rearview, and there's no use focusing on the past, only the present and what's coming.

Parenting is one of the most rewarding jobs. If done right, it is about being consistent, and consistency is the enemy of part-time. It's up to you what kind of parent you want to be: a part-time parent or a full-time parent who is a constant force in your child's life. Your kids will remember your parenting legacy forever, and how they turn out, good or bad, is largely up to how you parent.

Every chapter here outlines a clear theme and ends with a family challenge and an actionable parenting checklist. These ensure that you'll always have a battle plan for handling life's toughest moments as a family. There's also a whole section of parenting resources in the back of the book, full of reminders, tips, and suggestions to help you throughout your journey. With these tools, you won't just raise kids who can weather the storm; you'll raise self-reliant leaders, capable of charting their course and thriving in a world full of challenges. If you are consistent in using the following methods, you'll end up with incredible children who are independent, happy, and living a life filled with purpose.

And what parent wouldn't want that for their kids?

1

Cultivating Mental Strength

Do not pray for an easy life, pray for the strength to endure a difficult one.

—BRUCE LEE

Let's talk about Bruce Lee. He wasn't just a martial arts icon and cinematic legend; he was a philosopher in motion, a man who taught discipline, grit, and the power of self-awareness through every punch he threw and every word he spoke. He was also a father. The teachings he passed on to his students, fans, and kids weren't just about fighting; they were about living with purpose and confronting hardship with strength. His own daughter, Shannon Lee, remembers him as strict but loving and warm. Though Lee's words at the start of this chapter could easily apply to so many aspects of the human experience, they couldn't be more true than when it comes to parenting. Raising kids can feel like facing off in Bruce Lee's *Enter the Dragon*, surrounded, outnumbered, and one wrong move away from defeat.

What keeps our kids steady when the world tilts is mental toughness. Mental toughness is the ability to choose calmness and clarity when chaos erupts. In the SEAL Teams, especially as snipers, we trained our minds before we ever touched a firearm. Mental preparation was paramount. Parenting is no different: You either lead with calm clarity, ready for any situation, or you freak out amid the inevitable chaos. It's a conscious choice, and whatever you choose, you're modeling behavior for your children.

Mentally tough, emotionally sharp kids don't fall apart when life punches them in the mouth. And as we all know by now, life rarely pulls punches. Kids need independence, resilience, and the ability to stand strong in a world that won't always be kind to them when we're not around. Sure, we want to protect them from danger: bullying, mental health struggles, bad influences, violence, addiction, and the endless pull of digital screens. The weight of those fears can keep us parents up at night, wondering if we're doing enough, if we're getting it right. Worse, though, is when we default to overprotection.

In the early '90s, the University of Arizona created a biosphere project to mimic space colonization on Mars. Scientists lived and studied in a closed environment to learn how to exist on other planets. One of the most shocking discoveries was that the trees in the biosphere grew tall, but after a time, they would just fall over. Scientists found that, in order to build a firm foundation, the trees actually needed the stress from wind, which was absent inside the biosphere. Just as trees need stress to grow strong, so do our children. (Remember this the next time you're afraid to let your kid go on that overnight trip with friends or ride the subway by themselves.) Kids also need to be prepared to weather the storm of negativity in their everyday lives, especially in the age of social media and internet clickbait, where it flows like the Nile.

The antidote? Positivity—positive teaching, positive self-talk, and positive reinforcement. This trait can be developed through the same tools I learned and taught in sniper school—visualization, debriefs, and mindset drills—and have used to raise kids who don't crack under pressure.

A Life-Changing Call

I had just come off an intense combat mission hunting terrorists in the caves of northern Afghanistan. It was November 2001, not long after my deployment with SEAL Team 3 in the wake of the 9/11 attacks. When we returned to base, I got the message that my first son, Jackson, had been born. Excitement hit me at the same time as fear. All I could think about was surviving this deployment long enough to make it home and meet my new family.

A few months later, in February 2002, our SEAL platoon landed at Naval Air Station North Island in San Diego. Stepping off that cargo plane after months in the dust-choked mountains of Afghanistan felt surreal. One minute I was living out of a backpack in the dirt, the next I was surrounded by running water, clean streets, and a Starbucks on every corner.

For the first few weeks at home, Gretchen wouldn't leave me alone with our new tiny redheaded baby boy for fear I'd break him. She's always been a very protective mama bear, and I respect her for this—Gretchen is a great mom.

Soon, I was changing diapers with the speed and precision of a Formula 1 pit crew and settling into my new job as an advanced sniper instructor. I taught helicopter and urban sniper techniques to the West Coast SEAL Teams at the training command known as Sniper Cell, a small cadre of operationally seasoned instructors led by Jason Gardner, who would later become the command master chief of SEAL Team 5. It was a tough, tight group, and I thrived in that environment. At the same time, I had slipped into fatherhood more naturally than I had expected, determined to carry forward the best parts of my own upbringing while leaving the darker parts behind. Life felt balanced—hard training on one side and a growing family on the other. Then one early San Diego morning, the phone rang after my morning workout; I had just finished a four-mile jog on the cool and foggy Coronado beach by the office. It was a call that would set my life on a completely different course.

Sometimes life drops a fork in the road right in front of you—a moment, a decision—and you don't even realize it's happening until years later when you reflect on where you've ended up. That's the thing about turning points: They feel ordinary in real time, but they rewrite your entire history going forward. I had no clue this was one of those moments for me. But it was. Everything was about to change in a way I couldn't have imagined. Looking back now, that call probably saved my life.

The call was from Bob, a SEAL Team 6 senior chief and the kind of guy whose word carried real weight. He was running the SEAL basic course on the West Coast and asked if I'd come to augment the three-month-long SEAL sniper pilot course as a guest instructor. No big sales pitch. Just straight talk: "We could use you." But underneath that casual tone, I could tell this wasn't just another assignment. This was an opportunity. I could either lean in, step up, and say yes or play it safe and miss out on a potential shot. And I wasn't the play-it-safe type.

"Brandon," Bob said, "we really need your help with the new sniper course. We need guys with operational sniper experience to weigh in on the future of SEAL sniper training. I'd like to invite you to some amazing seminars on positive psychology and coaching. Then you'd join us for the first pilot course."

I was skeptically curious. In the Teams, we had no problem tearing down old methods if something better came along, but "positive psychology seminars" sounded more like corporate fluff than sniper school. Still, my curiosity and respect for Bob kept me listening.

Sniper Cell was a great place to work, and I wasn't sure I wanted to give that up to work for Bob. I was also looking forward to some downtime as a basic SEAL instructor after my tour at the Cell finished—"shore duty" as we say in the Navy. Whereas "sea duty" is at a high operational tempo, shore duty is a time to take a break. Think of it like working forty-hour weeks and being home in time for dinner every night versus ninety-hour weeks and being away from home all the time. I was craving a reduced work schedule; I was craving shore duty.

Once I became a SEAL instructor at BUD/S (Basic Underwater Demolition/SEAL training), I would only work a few days a week and get some needed downtime. Still, the days I worked were full throttle. BUD/S is divided into three phases, and each one is designed to forge something different in a cadet:

- First Phase is physical conditioning, the infamous freezing surf torture, endless miles of running in the soft sand, moving telephone poles up and down sand berms for fun, and of course, Hell Week (over five days of training with no sleep). It isn't about building muscle; it's about building grit. Candidates learn that the body will quit long before the mind, and those who make it are the ones who figure out how to suffer without giving in.
- Second Phase is dive training. Here, we take away control, comfort, and even oxygen. Candidates are pushed to the edge underwater, learning how to master panic and stay calm when everything in their bodies screams to bolt for the surface. It's a master class in focus and trust—trust in your gear, your buddy, and yourself.
- Third Phase is land warfare. This is where the skills start to look like combat: weapons, land navigation, demolitions, and small-unit tactics. It's about precision under pressure, decision-making amid utter commotion, and learning to fight as a team no matter the conditions.

Across all three phases, we teach much more than just how to shoot, dive, or blow things up. We teach resilience, clarity under stress, and how to keep moving forward when quitting looks like the easy out. Those are lessons that last a lifetime, whether you're on the battlefield or just trying to lead your family through the trials and tribulations of everyday life.

As you can imagine, each phase is intense, even for the instructors at times, but for me, it would still be shore duty. With my downtime, I planned on finishing my bachelor's degree, spending more time with my family, and getting my pilot's license after another year of teaching at Sniper Cell. However, Bob was strongly pushing me to leave Sniper Cell and my eventual BUD/S job to become a full-time sniper instructor, continuing ninety-hour work weeks and a grueling schedule.

He made his case. "The guys going downrange need you, Webb. You are one of the few snipers with actual combat experience," he said bluntly.

But I had a young family to think of. My son was still just a baby, and I had other thoughts on what was best for me. I figured I would at least humor Bob, though, and at the very minimum, I would join the course as a guest instructor this one time, then return to Sniper Cell, before transitioning to BUD/S as an instructor. I also thought I could at least add some operational wisdom to the program.

I told Bob I was in.

The Power of Positive Psychology

One of the seminars I attended before the pilot sniper program began would forever change my thinking, both as an instructor and as a father. An Olympic gold medalist sport shooter named Lanny Bassham spoke to us. Bassham had flopped during his first Olympics in Munich in 1972. He admitted, "It was the worst performance of my career, and I had already won the world championships and expected to win Olympic gold."

Instead, he won silver, but as he used to say, "Silver is just the first loser! Do you want to know what sucks even more? The worst thing about winning the silver medal is that everyone always asks me the same follow-up question: Who won gold?"

After losing the gold medal, Bassham sank into depression. "I totally lost it and did not know how it happened or how to manage the voice in my head," he told us all those years later in a small, dull Arizona hotel conference room. Then he started seeking the best sports psychologists to help him get over it and win. Bassham explained that all the psychologists he spoke to in the '70s just wanted to make him feel better about being a silver medalist, or a "loser," as he joked.

"There was no such thing as positive psychology back then," Bassham explained, "and I didn't want to be a happy loser; I wanted to be an Olympic champion!"

Confession: When I first heard about the seminar with Bassham, I thought, *Here we go again with some Tony Robbins jump up and down bullshit.* Years later, I would come to appreciate Robbins's philosophy, but back then, I had the overconfidence that a lot of young, cocky professionals have who've experienced some success early in life. I was about to find out how full of shit I really was.

The heartfelt stories and mental management lessons Bassham shared with us over the week would both surprise and humble me. One of the biggest takeaways came from Bassham's firsthand research. He'd interviewed all of the gold medalists on the US Olympic team over the course of a year and discovered that they had at least three traits in common:

- **Positive Self-Talk Routines.** These routines helped medalists become their own coach, replacing negative self-talk and negative thoughts with positive self-talk and positive thoughts. For example, instead of "I don't know if I can make a perfect shot," they would tell themselves, "It's like me to make a perfect shot."
- **Mental Rehearsal.** By mentally picturing a perfect shot, play, or move, they set themselves up to achieve their goal. They would close their eyes and imagine themselves practicing a skill perfectly while also rehearsing contingencies for when shit hit the fan, as it often does. (If you've seen *Drive to Survive* on Netflix, you'll notice the F1 drivers practicing laps on the track with their eyes closed.)

- **High Self-Images.** This self-confidence was based on their skill level, attained through thousands of hours of practice. In their minds, they were already winners, and they had the mindset that they would beat the competition even if severely handicapped. When they had a bad day training, they stopped and waited a day to begin again in order to avoid imprinting negative thoughts and performance or risk deflating their self-image.

Bassham used these common traits and other information he gleaned from the interviews to develop his own personal mental management program. He would then use this system during the 1976 Olympics in Montreal—where he took home the gold. (Bassham also wrote an amazing book I'd recommend for both you and your kids: *With Winning in Mind*. In the book, he details a simple and practical starter guide to learning and practicing mental management.)

These positive psychology lessons left a mark on me, and I carried them over when guest teaching at the sniper pilot program. Shortly after, Bob wound up convincing me to join the course as a full-time instructor. My promotion to course manager for the West Coast SEAL Teams came within six months, and less than a year later, I achieved the rank of chief petty officer, a significant milestone in the Navy, especially before turning thirty. The Navy had little choice in promoting me to chief. When I submitted my advancement package, I was already serving as the course manager with the rank of E6, and an E8 usually filled my job, or senior chief petty officer, two ranks higher than me.

Becoming a chief at such a young age was a moment of pride, and to borrow the words of the legendary LA philosopher Snoop Dogg, "I'd like to thank me." It was one of those rare times I let myself fully acknowledge the thirteen years of hard work and grit it took to get there since joining the Navy. And after becoming the head sniper instructor, I decided to fully integrate mental management into our curriculum—the results came fast.

> **Take a Break**
>
> Just as the world's greatest Olympians pause and wait a day to resume training when they've hit a wall, when your kid is having a bad day, it's often best to take a break. Think about your kid struggling with their math homework. If they're exhausted and frustrated, pushing them harder only locks in the feeling that they "can't do it." Instead, step back. Let them sleep on it, reset, and return fresh the next day. You'll be surprised how often the problem solves itself once their mind isn't carrying the baggage of failure.

Positive Teaching

In the past, we'd had a sink-or-swim attitude as instructors, because that was the way it had always been done. If the students didn't learn to drink water from the sniper fire hose, we'd fail them and send them back to their SEAL Teams, having removed their sniper fins. The sniper program was one of the most stressful, feared, and respected programs in the Teams. It is also one of the few courses you can fail in the Teams and not lose your SEAL Trident. But ninety days is a serious time commitment for a Team to send a SEAL for training, so if someone didn't make it, they would rarely get another shot.

The core principle I started using in the sniper program was the power of a positive teaching style over negative feedback loops. In the past, my fellow instructors and I employed a negative style of instruction. We would verbalize how badly the students were messing up, and we'd be quick to tell them. "Stop fucking flinching on the trigger, Johnny!" we'd yell on the firing line. This negative feedback would spread like COVID down the line, infecting all the other students. Now the idea of "flinching" filled every student's thoughts. This was essentially programming students with negativity and setting them up for ongoing failure.

When you are teaching a beginner, especially a young child, it's incredibly important to positively imprint desired outcomes or behavior—not reinforce the negatives. Unfortunately, as parents, we often focus on those negatives. For example, how many times have you heard parents shout, "Stop yelling!" instead of saying, "Please be quiet"? Beginners are like a blank canvas, and you paint a picture of either success or failure; it's that simple.

Positive Feedback and Positive Self-Talk

Rather than verbalize mistakes, with the new system, we'd give only positive corrective feedback. Instead of barking, "Stop flinching as you pull the trigger!" we'd give a direct positive command: "Take a deep breath, exhale, and pull smoothly." Two entirely different mental pictures—the latter influences the desired outcome, whereas the former is just bad mental programming.

I also wanted to change the way we set glass ceiling limits through verbalization. For example, I altered the way we spoke about tests to influence students' positive self-talk. Students would inevitably ask what constituted a good score on a shooting test—80 percent was the minimum passing grade. But when I employed the new system, I said to the instructors, "Do not tell them anything short of perfect. Let them know when they ask (they always do) that a good score is a perfect 100 percent." After we implemented this standard, something remarkable happened: Students started shooting perfect scores for the first time.

Further, we showed students how to change negative self-talk into positive self-talk through mantras and mental checklists. For example, a student might catch themself thinking, "I always screw this shot up. I can't get it right." That spiral eats away at confidence. We trained them to replace it with "Breathe. Relax. Focus. Smooth trigger squeeze." Over time, those words became automatic—a mental checklist that left no room for doubt. In the process, the positive self-talk actually pushed out the negative self-talk.

It's the same with kids. When they start saying, "I'm terrible at science" or "I'll never make the team," we can help them reframe: "I'm learning this step-by-step" or "I'll give my best effort today." Just like the sniper student, the positive script becomes their default, forcing out the negative before it takes root.

With my own kids, I discussed the importance of recognizing well-meaning, misinformed adults who use negative criticism and how to turn that negative feedback into positive self-talk. It was important for me to explain that not everyone out there knows how to build people up. Some teachers, coaches, and even family members think the only way to help you improve is by pointing out everything you're doing wrong. They highlight mistakes and negativity without thinking about it because they don't know any better. But that just puts negative thoughts and energy into kids' heads and causes them to burn out before they ever even catch fire.

Whenever someone comes at us with negative feedback, we need to make a habit of flipping that feedback in our heads. If someone says, "You'll never get that right," we tell ourselves, "I'm learning. I'll figure this out." If they say, "That was terrible," we say, "That was practice." If you hear, "Don't miss the net!" or "Don't strike out!" we say, "Put it into the goal!" or "Hit it out of the park!"

Kids shouldn't believe every single thing adults say about them, especially if it doesn't help them get closer to their goal. Instead, they've got to become their own coach at times, learning how to replace negative thoughts and negative self-talk with positive thoughts and positive self-talk. Encourage them to do the following: When they hear something negative, tell them to pause, take a breath, and say, "That's one opinion, not the final word." Then help them reframe it with their own positive take. That's how they get stronger, both mentally and physically.

Everyday Reframes for Raising Mentally Tough Kids

A study by the Gottman Institute at the University of Washington found that for every one negative interaction, a child needs at least five positive ones to maintain emotional stability. That means every time you or another adult barks at your kid or shoots down their idea, it takes five moments of genuine connection just to get them back to neutral. Stack enough negatives, and you're not building resilience; you're breaking trust.

The everyday inputs we give our kids—our words, our tone, our expectations—matter more than most people realize. Over time, negative input wears them down like water running over stones. Positive, constructive input builds them up like forging steel. If all they hear is where they're falling short, they start believing they're not capable. But when they get consistent, honest encouragement alongside the correction? That's when they step into their full potential.

You see it everywhere once you start paying attention, people casually beating themselves down without even realizing it: "I'm not good with numbers." "I'm just not athletic." "I'm a klutz." "I could never do that." It's like we're all carrying around this quiet negative loop in the back of our minds, repeating old stories someone else planted there years ago. Maybe it was a teacher, a coach, or a parent who didn't know any better. But over time, that kind of talk becomes automatic. People start believing their own limitations as if they're facts instead of habits. It emerges in the smallest ways in kids, like shrugging off new challenges, backing away from opportunity, or quitting before they even start. And unless you catch it and flip that script, it becomes a self-fulfilling prophecy. This is why it's so important to teach our kids to develop a positive self-image from a young age.

Here are some examples you can use to think about reframing language to support, instead of inhibit, your children:

Instead of: "That's just not who you are."
→ Say: "You get to decide who you are, one choice at a time."

Instead of: "You failed."
→ Say: "You found one way that didn't work. That's progress."

Instead of: "Don't embarrass yourself."
→ Say: "The only real loss is not showing up."

Instead of: "I told you so."
→ Say: "Looks like we learned something the hard way. That sticks better, doesn't it?"

Instead of: "You're too young to understand."
→ Say: "Let me break this down for you. You're old enough to learn."

Instead of: "That's not my problem."
→ Say: "Let's figure out a solution together. What's your first move?"

Instead of: "You'll regret that."
→ Say: "Before you decide, picture how you'll feel about it tomorrow."

Instead of: "That's just the way it is."
→ Say: "Things are the way we make them. Let's change the outcome."

Instead of: "You're making a mess of this."

→ Say: "Every pro was once a beginner. Stay in it."

Instead of: "Don't cry."

→ Say: "It's OK to feel it. Then we stand back up and get after it."

Visualization

A young Navy pilot, Jack Sands, was downed during the Vietnam War. After being captured, Sands was a prisoner of war under brutal conditions for over four years. The American POWs called the camp in which he was held the "Hanoi Hilton." I've been through POW training, and it was one of the hardest experiences of my military life outside of sniper school and SEAL training. The first thing they do in a POW camp is strip you of your identity. In training, I was no longer Brandon Webb. I was war criminal number 53. In a small concrete box, I lived, endured torture, ate, and defecated in a cheap coffee tin for close to a week. So I can only imagine what it was like to spend years in a hell like this. But Sands did it, and throughout, he used visualization as a mental escape mechanism.

An avid golfer, Sands would close his eyes and play all his favorite Navy courses over and over in his mind. He'd visualize hitting a perfect drive down the fairway, then, using an iron, he'd blast the ball onto the green in another shot and put fifteen yards straight into the hole for a birdie. Sands played perfect golf in his head for those four-plus years.

After being liberated from the prison camp when the war ended, Sands landed back at Naval Air Station San Diego. He and his fellow POWs were bused over the Coronado Bridge to the Balboa Naval Hospital for a checkup, but Sands never made it—as the bus passed the North Island golf course, he threw a fit and made the driver let him off so he could shoot a round of golf.

Everyone thought he was crazy, especially as he walked onto the course to play. After being refused entry because of his disheveled looks, he introduced himself to his fellow Navy comrades, and with tears in their eyes, they outfitted him in the pro shop to play a round.

And you know what?

He shot eighteen holes par.

When everyone expressed shock, he replied something like "Fellas, I don't know what to tell you, I've been playing perfect golf in my head for four years!"

Visualization was another technique we began using to train and encourage our students. I had a pair of students named Ted and Adam who were particularly interested in this approach. Recognizing their enthusiasm, I loaned them a Bassham CD (back when we had those things!) on the topic. After a long day of training, they'd listen to it in their rental car, which had a CD player. I remember overhearing the other classmates making fun of them: "Hey Ted, you and Adam going to make out in the car again tonight?"

On the first day of testing with semiautomatic rifles, they each had two tests. Pop-up and moving targets at unknown distances out to 800 meters require rapid distance and wind calculations. Ted scored 100 percent on both, and Adam scored 100 and 95. That meant Ted hit forty out of forty shots perfectly, and Adam dropped only one shot. My instructors and the students were speechless. I guess those make-out sessions paid off. Needless to say, those Bassham CDs became very popular among our students! It was a proud moment for me and a huge confidence booster for Ted, Adam, and the rest of the class, who were skeptical that such positive psych techniques were valid.

My students also learned to use visualization to rehearse emergency contingencies when things go wrong. Whether it was a bad wind or a last-minute elevation adjustment that could throw off their entire shot, they would practice what to do in that moment, quickly making the needed correction in their heads. We see this in elite sports as well. For example, during the 100-meter butterfly Olympic finals in Beijing in 2008, Michael Phelps dove into the pool when the starting gun went off. As he entered the water, however, his goggles came loose and flooded out entirely, blinding him. Phelps could have panicked, but he had already mentally rehearsed for this emergency, and his training kicked in. He immediately started counting his strokes, something he imagined in his head over and over again. The result? He not only won the race but also set a new world record, all with flooded goggles.

As my students' experience and these examples prove, visualization works, and it can be an edge for your kids in many aspects of their lives. The same mental management principles I taught to snipers, I used on my own children. For example, there was a time when my oldest son, Jackson, had to get up in front of his elementary school class to give a talk, and he was terrified. He's not alone: Comedian Jerry Seinfeld claimed in one of his bits, "According to most studies, people's number one fear is public speaking. Number two is death. Death is number two . . . This means to the average person, if you go to a funeral, you're better off in the casket than doing the eulogy." (In reality, about 77 percent of people have at least some fear of public speaking.) I showed Jackson how to visualize the experience over and over in his head to get rid of his nerves. Years later, he was recognized as an Academic All-American for his high school speech and debate team accomplishments.

I also remember the first time my daughter used visualization for a downhill ski race in Oregon when she was on the high school team. "This stuff really works, Dad!" she beamed with a huge smile after putting up the fastest downhill time. Guiding your kids through this type of effective mental rehearsal is a powerful skill they will carry with them for the rest of their lives.

The Results

Typically, a sniper course would last three months, with seven days a week of intense training in field craft, stalking, ballistics, advanced weaponry, and more. The course eliminated 30 percent of the class on average. What happened when I taught the mental management course in the first week of sniper training? We graduated *everyone*, and the rate stayed there throughout the course—30 percent to 0 percent! Occasionally, we'd lose someone who just couldn't put it all together, but that was incredibly rare.

My instructors and I saw how switching to a positive teaching style worked better than a negative one. The proof was in front of our faces every day with our students' performance on the range and in the classroom. Not only did our graduation rate shoot up to nearly 100 percent for the first time in the program's history, but we had several students in class consistently scoring perfectly on their shooting exams, also a first. My experiment with teaching mental management was paying off, and the daily results were proof that using these techniques worked. This wasn't something that took time to see; it happened the moment we changed our course material.

We couldn't believe the success rate because we'd also made the sniper course harder when I took over. The program was more technically challenging, and the shooting tests were incredibly difficult, but we still graduated with record numbers of snipers, which was great news for the SEAL community—and terrible news for the bad guys downrange.

I remember receiving calls from SEAL Teams to compliment our achievements with their snipers—but they weren't the only ones. SEAL snipers loaned to the Army in Iraq and Afghanistan displayed exacting efficiency on every mission, and the commanders took notice—a few Army unit commanders in Iraq even called to ask my instructors about our sniper program's curriculum material. Appreciate the rare circumstances of an Army guy calling a

Navy guy to heap praise—that just doesn't happen often. And it was the best compliment I could ever ask for as the head instructor of the sniper program.

I'm also proud to report that snipers we trained through the program have gone on to use these skills to incredible success in other areas. You may have heard of the former Navy SEAL turned Harvard doctor and NASA astronaut Johnny Kim. He is a graduate of the modern SEAL sniper program, and I'd like to think his time at sniper school helped prepare him for where he is today.

The type of mindset and practice regimen we instilled in our students separates the champions from the crowd. But here's the truth: Champions aren't just born on podiums; they're raised in kitchens, backyards, and driveways. They're shaped by the little nudges, the quiet pep talks, and the moments when someone believes in them more than they believe in themselves. That's why the way we speak to our kids matters so much. Every word we choose, especially when things get hard, can either build a bridge over the rough patches or make those patches feel like walls.

Case Study: Carol Dweck's Growth Mindset Research

Psychologist Carol Dweck's work on the growth mindset is amazing. It feels like she's unlocked a secret parenting weapon for success. Her research is a game-changer and proves my point on the power of mental management in parenting. Dweck and her team ran a simple but eye-opening experiment with schoolchildren. They gave two groups a set of puzzles to solve. Afterward, they praised one group for their intelligence, saying, "You're so smart!" They praised the other group for their effort: "You worked hard on that!"

What happened next is where it gets interesting. When offered a choice between trying a harder puzzle or sticking with an easier one, the "smart" kids were more likely to stay with the easier option—they didn't want to risk looking dumb. The "effort" kids were more likely to choose the harder puzzle. They saw challenges as opportunities to grow rather than threats to their egos. Over time, this mindset difference snowballed. The kids praised for their efforts developed resilience, grit, and a hunger to learn. The "smart" kids? They started avoiding challenges altogether, afraid to fail and tarnish their identity as "gifted."

The lesson here is crystal clear: As parents, our words shape how our kids see themselves. If we focus on praising outcomes, grades, trophies, or wins, we risk creating kids who are terrified of failure. But if we praise the process, the hustle, the grit, the lessons learned, we raise kids who run toward challenges, not away from them.

Champions aren't just cultivated in training fields or classrooms; they're built in the ordinary moments at home, in the words that echo the loudest when kids are struggling. The stories our kids tell themselves start with the stories we tell them. Negative talk, whether it's "You're not good at this" or "Why can't you get it right?" constructs walls in their heads that they'll spend years trying to climb. Positive talk—praising effort, grit, and the courage to try again—builds bridges that carry them over setbacks and into growth.

That's the power of mental management in parenting. Every word is a seed. Plant fear, and kids will avoid challenges. Plant resilience, and they'll chase them. What we say when things get hard doesn't just change the moment; it shapes who our kids believe they can become.

Field Note: How We Talk Matters

- Your voice becomes your children's inner voice. The way you talk to your kids—especially in the tough moments—sets the tone for how they'll talk to themselves for the rest of their lives.

- Replace the negative loop. When the words in their head turn against them, give them the tools—mantras, visualization, reframing—to change the channel.
- Praise the process, not the label. "You worked hard on that" builds grit. "You're so smart" builds fear of failure.

Family Challenge: Let your child try something new this week with no rescue plan—line up one trusted adult to cheer them on when they complete the task.

Advice from Tyler: *Take your kids traveling when they're young, even if it's just to new cities or unfamiliar settings. It helps them get comfortable being uncomfortable, which builds the resilience they'll need when life throws them curveballs, like switching schools. New places teach kids how to adapt, adjust, and grow.*

Chapter Checklist

- **Use Positive Framing.** Avoid negative instructions ("Don't yell"). Replace with positive phrasing ("Use a calm voice, please").
- **Visualize Success.** Help your child picture the best outcome ("Imagine yourself speaking in front of class. How will you feel? Is there anything we can mentally rehearse for now to make the speech go better for you?"). Guide your child through a visualization exercise of succeeding in upcoming challenges.
- **Encourage Positive Self-Talk.** Replace phrases like "I'm not good at this" with a new mantra (write this down somewhere): "I'm learning, and I'll get better."
- **Reinforce Identity.** Use affirmations to strengthen their self-image ("You're the kind of person who works hard and finishes what you start").
- **Pause and Redirect Negative Feedback.** Instead of focusing on your kids' mistakes, highlight what they did well and how they can improve ("Great effort on your math test; next time, you can ask me for help if you need it").
- **Model Resilience.** Share examples of how you have overcome setbacks using positive mental strategies.
- **Celebrate Wins.** Acknowledge progress, big or small, to build confidence and reinforce good habits.

2

Building Confidence

Children must be taught how to think, not what to think, and failure is one of the best teachers.

—MARGARET MEAD

Margaret Mead was a groundbreaking twentieth-century American cultural anthropologist whose work reshaped how we understand childhood, parenting, and the power of the environment in shaping human behavior. Her research reminded us that children aren't meant to be protected from struggle—they're meant to be shaped by it. Every time a child fails, it's an opportunity for them to grow. Shield them from failure, and you steal their chance to learn resilience, grit, and self-confidence.

However, you should never let them believe that failure means they're broken. That's the difference between raising someone who needs approval and someone who builds their own damn ladder. I learned that lesson twice: once during my time as a Navy SEAL and once again when my daughter Madison shared something that struck me right between the eyes. When she was twenty and finishing undergrad at Goldsmiths, I asked her what she wished I'd done differently as her father. She told me she wished she'd heard more about the times when I had stumbled throughout my life. The real stuff. The screwups, the setbacks, the moments I doubted myself. Her words reminded me that vulnerability isn't weakness—it's connection. And if we want our kids to be strong, they need to see where our cracks are too. Not just the medals, but the bruises.

Mistakes? I've got a filing cabinet full. My biggest regret? Tanking my high school grades and killing my shot at a good college with ROTC. I had my heart set on being a Navy fighter pilot, but instead I ended up taking the scenic route—straight into Navy search and rescue, then BUD/S and the SEAL Teams. Another regret? Writing my memoir, *The Red Circle*, without fully thinking through the blast radius. I told my truth, but it rattled everyone from former SEAL teammates to my own father. I was radically transparent and honest, but most people, as Jack Nicholson famously said, "can't handle the truth." That's me—mess up, move on, and don't linger in the wreckage. The problem is, when you don't share those wrecks with your kids, they grow up thinking they're the only ones who've ever been in a ditch.

What nobody writes about in those sanitized parenting books—featuring soft pastel covers and titles like *Raising Rainbows* and *Every Kid Wins!*—is that parenting is a full-contact sport. You have to allow, and even sometimes position, your kids to be in situations that will challenge them with failure and adversity. Like the Hindus say, gold becomes pure only after being forged in fire. Our children are no different.

When I was a kid, I didn't learn confidence from praise. Instead, I got a fateful face-punch lesson in adversity, and I have my father to thank for it. At sixteen, I got kicked off my family's boat—literally and metaphorically. We were on a family sailing trip halfway around the world, and my father and I had a big blow-up when we hit landfall in Tahiti. There's nothing quite like staring into the South Pacific with a busted ego, a half-packed bag, a few hundred dollars to your name, and the existential question, What the hell just happened to my life?

By thirteen, I had already earned my sea legs, working long days on a scuba diving boat based out of Ventura Harbor in California. The ocean was in my blood, the gray deck under my feet as familiar as my own bedroom floor. By the age of sixteen, I'd logged more hours on and under the water than most adults. At the time, my father was working middle management in a construction company, and my mother, always adventurous, was cooking on the offshore drilling platforms in the Channel Islands. They'd finally saved up enough for us to set out on our second big sailing adventure as a family, ready for whatever the ocean threw our way, and there would be plenty. The problem was that I was a cocky teen who was about to learn an important lesson: There can be only one captain on a ship—and that captain was my dad.

I can't recall the exact words that pushed my father into full-blown DEFCON One, but whatever they were, I'd been feeding that fire for a while. One moment we were circling each other, snapping like two pit bulls straining against short chains; the next, he was in my face, fist drawn back like Zeus ready to hurl a bolt from the heavens. My mother's eyes went wide—a look that said, *Oh God, they're really going to do it*—and for a heartbeat, I wasn't sure she was wrong. But we didn't. And when the storm passed, like Ice Cube said back in the day, we both knew what time it was.

One captain per ship, right?

In a final act of dramatic restraint, he told me to pack my crap and get off his boat. Not *our* boat, *his* boat. Like I was some stowaway bum who'd outworn his welcome. No punches. No drama. Just a terrifying calm that meant he'd already made up his mind.

I was sixteen. Alone. In need of passage back to America. This wasn't some after-school special TV show. This was real life. I had to figure it out.

And I did.

I hitched a ride with a family on a forty-foot catamaran bound for Hilo, Hawai'i, 3,000 miles away. The couple and their toddler needed an extra crewman for the night watch. I needed a lift. The trade worked. I stood midnight shifts under a cathedral of stars, sailing alone with my thoughts, trade winds blowing warmly on my face as I wrestled with fear, grief, and the soul-splintering realization that my safety net was gone. My childhood was suddenly over.

I won't lie—I broke down in tears of angst those first few nights. Ever try shouting into the ocean? The Pacific doesn't flinch. It just keeps rolling, cold and unforgiving. That was my reality check. But slowly, somewhere between fear and freedom, I found something else—the first spark of true confidence.

There's a strange thing that happens when you're out in the void, no backup, no plan B. You either break or grow stronger, die a victim or sharpen into a weapon. I wasn't ready to break. And I knew I wasn't a victim.

That trip to Hawai'i became a crucible for me. I made it to Hilo, then flew commercial back to the mainland. When I got home, the owner of the boat I grew up working on, Bill Magee, took me in. Bill was more than just my boss—he had long been a mentor to me as well. He was also the kind of guy who didn't ask questions; he just gave me my job back and handed me a bunk to sleep in.

Boat life became my life again. And for the first time, I realized something no self-help book or participation trophy could teach: Confidence doesn't come from being comfortable. It comes from getting wrecked and building yourself back up without anyone holding your hand.

Confidence isn't a state of mind—it's a skillset forged in fire.

Help Them Crawl, Walk, Then Run . . .

Now, do I suggest that the best way to build confidence is to drop your kid off by themselves halfway around the world and let them sink or swim? Not quite. But there are times to untie our kids so they can set off on their own journey and experience their own struggle. This could be walking to the bus stop for the first time by themselves, going to a sleepaway camp, or taking a solo trip overseas.

When it comes to building confidence, there's no better way than the crawl, walk, run method—help them start small and slowly build a strong foundation of achievement. This can be done in a variety of ways and can come in all shapes and sizes: sports, martial arts, chess club, band, outdoor camp, travel, speech and debate competitions, and much more.

When my kids were barely out of the womb, one of the first things I taught them was how to swim. Swimming is one of the greatest skills you can teach a young child. If you start early enough, it becomes second nature, something that lives in their bones. Back in San Diego, Gretchen and I brought Jackson and Madison to a private infant swim school where they start babies as young as three months old in calm 93°F water. The whole "soft-touch, no-fear" approach resonated with us. They would take infants and gently dunk them under water, keeping their eyes open, and slowly teach them to swim with only their arms. It was incredible to see how fast they adapted. At just one year old, they were competent swimmers, diving to the bottom of the pool to retrieve objects. By the time Tyler was born, I'd watched and learned enough to teach him myself in our community pool. Seeing the mix of uncertainty and pride on their faces in those early days was worth every second.

When COVID hit, rather than lock ourselves indoors, I flew all three kids to Old San Juan, Puerto Rico, where I was hunkered down during the global pandemic. I found a crusty Army Special Forces diver named Jim at a local shop and had him run all three kids through the PADI (Professional Association of Diving Instructors) Advanced Open Water certification. I'll never forget hovering a hundred feet down, watching them fin past me with sea turtles like they owned the ocean. After they aced their lessons, Jim nodded and said, "Damn, your kids can swim." That's when it clicked—this was the payoff for teaching them early. Little skills taught young don't just stick; they stack. And one day, they turn into the kind of quiet confidence that can handle anything.

Bikes were the same story. I had all three kids riding early because I still remembered what it was like to have my own bike as a kid growing up in the '80s. It wasn't just transportation—it was independence. My bike meant I could explore my world on my own terms, without asking for a ride or waiting for someone to say yes. I knew I wanted my kids to have that sense of freedom as well.

Another way to start small, especially when your kids are young, is to have pets around. Pets can work wonders for a child's confidence and emotional development. A 2017 study published in *Anthrozoös*, a journal that explores the relationships between people and animals, found that children who had strong bonds with their dogs reported higher levels of self-esteem and lower levels of loneliness. Other research has found that pets, especially dogs, help kids develop empathy, emotional regulation, and social skills. The Human-Animal Bond Research Institute has even shown that pets provide a nonjudgmental presence that supports both emotional and cognitive growth. In plain English: The family dog doesn't care if your kid stumbles over their words or has a tough day at school—they still love them, and that kind of unconditional support is priceless for a child's self-image.

In our case, Riley, our golden retriever, was the kids' first furry anchor. From the moment we brought Jackson home, Riley wagging at his feet, I saw it: a child moored by unconditional love and curiosity. Later, when the kids moved with their mom to a ranch in Paso Robles, California, after the divorce, they found themselves surrounded by chickens, alpacas, dogs, cats, rabbits, and more. One afternoon, Madison jokingly named the last surviving chicken on the ranch "Lone Survivor," a nod to my friend Marcus Luttrell's book. That little name said it all—animals don't just teach responsibility; they spark humor, connection, and resilience.

On the ranch, each animal became a teacher: A rabbit taught patience, a cat taught grace, Lone Survivor taught humor, and Riley continued to teach loyalty with every sloppy kiss. Caring for pets—feeding them, watching them, feeling them lean in when you're upset—shows a kid they matter and can be trusted, and they can give trust in return.

But Let Them Fall Along the Way

Whether your child is at the stage of crawling, walking, or running, as discussed in chapter 1, if you are overprotective, you will push them into incompetence. Remember the biosphere trees? Emotional coddling stunts children when they're let out in the real world. To build a confident kid, put some weight on their back. Let them carry something. Let them earn something. Praise is good, but it doesn't build confidence; achievement through struggle does. And achievement only comes after a solid face-plant into the pavement of failure.

When my son Jackson was around twelve, he broke his arm going off a ski jump. I didn't coddle him. I gave him a high five instead. "You really went for it, huh?" I said, looking over at him as I drove him to the medical clinic to get his arm cast. I can still picture the big smile spread across his face. He knew he sent it, and it felt good, broken arm and all.

We don't need kids who play it safe. We need kids who learn by overcoming fear. Because fear isn't something to avoid; it's something to develop a familiarity with. Our children need to understand that both fear and failure are necessary parts of achievement.

Don't confuse this approach with being cold and unfeeling. Just as confidence doesn't come from being coddled, it doesn't come from being yelled at or belittled either. Confidence is the result of knowing that someone believes in you enough to let you earn it and that the same person will be there when things go bad, as they most certainly will at times. Your kids need space to fail, but you should never abandon them in the wreckage. Just stand by with your metaphorical first aid kit ready to say, "Get back in there, champ."

We live in a society that's become drunk on praise. Everyone gets a banner and a cupcake simply for showing up. Now we're seeing the negative side of this failed experiment: kids who expect rewards for effort alone and who collapse when the stakes rise. Similar to

Carol Dweck's research discussed in chapter 1, a long-term study by developmental psychology researcher Elizabeth Gunderson and her colleagues found that toddlers who were praised for their effort and strategies—not for being "smart"—grew into kids who were more resilient, were more eager to take on challenges, and performed better academically years later. The lesson is clear: Empty praise sets kids up for fragile confidence, while effort-based praise builds grit.

The real world doesn't hand out trophies for no reason; it rewards results. So if your kid loses the soccer game and comes home crying, don't lie and tell them they were amazing. Tell them, "Yeah, you lost. And it sucks. Losing is part of learning. So what are you gonna do about it?" Then teach them how to train smarter, work harder, and come back swinging.

For the first two years after Jackson joined the debate team, he lost every debate and never made it to a single final. Then during his junior year, something happened; he started winning everything. When we talked about this shift over dinner recently, he told me what a valuable lesson this was for him in perseverance. It helped him lay the foundation for a lifelong appreciation of how much practice, effort, and time it truly takes to become an expert.

As much as a lot of kids and parents want the "cheat code," you can't become a bona fide expert by skipping the line. There is no substitute for grinding it out through hard work and practice. Allow your kids to get into situations that let them experience failure. And then support them so they can rise up like a phoenix with scraped knees and a defiant smirk.

Case Study: The Minnesota Competence Enhancement Project

The Minnesota Competence Enhancement Project, led by Dr. Ann Masten at the University of Minnesota, spent years following kids who faced some of life's toughest challenges, including poverty, family upheaval, and other personal traumas. What Dr. Masten and her team wanted to uncover was simple: What helps some children not just survive adversity but actually come out stronger and more self-assured on the other side?

The answer wasn't constant hand-holding. Instead, Dr. Masten's research found that resilience and confidence grow out of the everyday experiences of taking on responsibility, facing real challenges, and having the chance to fail and try again, all with the steady support of caring adults. (Please read this twice so it sinks in.)

Dr. Masten calls these everyday confidence-building experiences *ordinary magic*, which is also the title of her book on the subject. In her research, kids who were trusted to handle meaningful tasks—like looking after siblings, helping with family chores, or making decisions that mattered—developed a deep sense of competence and belief in themselves. Through such experiences, they learned that they could weather life's storms and figure them out, even when things got tough. This ordinary magic is extremely powerful, but it's only possible if we learn to get out of the way and let it happen.

Ordinary Magic

The idea of "ordinary magic" hits home for me so strongly because I've seen it play out in my own family time and again. The science lines up perfectly with what I've witnessed as a parent: Confidence isn't built in a bubble; it's developed in those everyday moments when our kids are allowed to stretch, stumble, and stand back up on their own two feet. As parents, we have to always be on the hunt for the ordinary magic, those little daily moments that look like nothing from the outside but have the potential to build something big on the inside.

I'm not talking about orchestrated, Instagram-worthy milestones. I'm talking about the moments when you hand your kid a shovel or recipe book instead of a screen. Or when you challenge them to plan and lead the way on a family hike. Every one of those small tests adds up. They allow you to build your child's capability without a boring parent lecture and foster confidence without clapping.

Dr. Masten's research and my own experience both point to the same truth: When we trust our kids with real responsibility and let them navigate life's bumps with our support—not our interference—they develop lasting confidence. That's the "ordinary magic" I want for my children and for yours. Let me give you a few examples of how I've seen this magic come to life over the years.

Madison's Purple Taekwondo Belt

Paso Robles is a small town, so Gretchen and I always looked for positive activities for the kids. When she saw a sign for a new Taekwondo studio opening, we both thought it was a good idea to get them into martial arts. I practiced Taekwondo as a kid; it taught me a lot about self-discipline, and it was a huge confidence booster. I hoped it might do the same for the kids.

In the first year, both Jackson and Madison got their yellow belts (Tyler was too young to attend at the time), and I made the five-hour drive to visit when it was time for them to test for purple. The students' parents all filed into the studio housed inside a prefabricated metal building that smelled like a sweat-and-rust scented candle. Black padded mats covered the floor, and an American flag hung above the mirrors lining the front wall. The students stood in formation with their backs to us parents until the instructor gave the call to start their tests, facilitated by the black belt students. With a group bow, we were off.

Each kid got up in front of the room (talk about pressure!) to show their strikes and defensive techniques, demonstrating how they had mastered the next belt level. As a parent, you know how terrifying it can be to have your little ones judged by others, not to mention how these kids feel knowing that an audience of parents and their peers is watching their every move.

After what seemed like an eternity, the head of the school had the students sit and then critiqued them one by one. If they were successful, they stood up and walked to the instructor, who handed over the new belt. The student would then bow, take the new belt, and return to their seat. They finally arrived at Jackson, critiqued his performance, and asked him to come forward—he got his purple belt. Next up, it was his sister's turn. Madison was told to stand up. The instructor explained what she had done well but also that she had missed some of her key moves and would therefore not be awarded her next belt that day.

As a father watching this all unfold, I was terrified for Madison but also proud of her for keeping her composure. She was only ten years old. She nodded and sat back down stoically.

How could they embarrass my little girl in front of the entire school?

When I calmed down, I realized how valuable a life lesson this could be for me as a parent and for my daughter. I told Gretchen I'd drive Maddie home separately so I could talk with her. I could see the relief in Gretchen's face.

Madison made it into the passenger seat in my Tacoma, strapped her seat belt across her lap, and burst into tears. "But Jackson got his purple belt, and I didn't get mine, Dad," she sobbed.

"Madison, not everyone wins the first time," I explained. "Sometimes we fail, and how we deal with that failure will define our future outcomes negatively or positively. Work hard the next few weeks, and you'll be able to retest like your instructor said, and you'll know what it's like to earn it."

She said, "OK, Dad," as she wiped the tears from her eyes. I gave her a big hug, then took her for Mexican food, her favorite.

Madison didn't earn her belt that day, and as much as I wanted to swoop in and fix it for her, I knew that disappointment was a necessary part of her growth. But looking back, this was one of those moments I wish I could rewind. I should have opened up to her and let her see my own cracks, sharing my stories of falling short—not just once, but again and again—so she'd know failure isn't a dead end but a detour on the way forward. I could have told her about losing my first start-up and with it my entire life savings, about the nights I sat on the floor wondering how I'd dig out, and about how I eventually stood back up and rebuilt. I could have reminded her that even her Navy SEAL dad has stumbled hard, missed targets, and gotten it wrong. As my great friend Marco from Madrid likes to say, "Nobody is perfect." He's right—but we can be perfectly honest, and that's what our kids need most.

It's incredibly tough to see your children go through failure and hard to resist the parenting instinct to protect them at all costs, but failure is, at times, necessary. Winston Churchill said it best: "Never let a good tragedy go to waste!" Remember that the next time you have the urge to shield them.

I still have the image of the photo her mom texted me a few weeks later burned into memory: Madison dressed in her white *gi*, holding her new purple belt with a huge smile. She earned it, and it felt good.

Way to go, Maddie!

Tyler's Lesson in Teamwork

Tyler had a huge growth spurt the summer before he started high school. Over six feet tall and a solid basketball player, he was expected to make JV or even Varsity in his freshman year. After tryouts, he made the JV team, but he was about to learn an important lesson in humility—within a few weeks, he was kicked off for his attitude.

According to the coach, Tyler was unfocused at practice, and he arrived at every one with a huge chip on his shoulder, which immediately got knocked off when he was given the boot. "Tyler is my best freshman," the coach explained, "but he's setting a bad example for the rest of his teammates. He doesn't listen. So I'm replacing him with a player who will."

As someone who's coached youth baseball, I know how terrible and unreasonable parents can be toward coaches, especially when their kids are put in a tough spot like this. I've seen parents tear into coaches trying to defend their kids' actions, as if their children were incapable of bad behavior, but this parental attitude only further contributes to creating little monsters.

After verifying the facts with Gretchen about what had happened, she and I were on the same page about letting Tyler take responsibility for his mistake. It would have been easy for us to call the principal or push it with the coach, but we knew this wouldn't teach Tyler anything meaningful. He was shocked that he had been canned from the team, and he tried to apologize his way back in. But the coach's mind was already made up, and he'd quickly given Tyler's spot away.

Tyler had to go the full school year watching his basketball buddies play games he should have been in. It was torture for him—but it was also humbling. When we spoke privately over dinner about the importance of being a team player, I shared my experiences in SEAL training about the talented jerks who ended up quitting or getting kicked out of the Team and sent back to the Navy for not earning their SEAL Trident pin every day.

I told Tyler the story of my swim buddy Rob in BUD/S training. He was an incredibly smart, talented athlete, and he excelled at everything thrown his way, but he was also cocky and selfish. At the end of our three months of SEAL tactical training, before we were assigned a SEAL platoon as new guys, Rob got his own lesson in humility, along with a nice dose of karma.

Our class was on the final stretch of the program, and we were about to finish our final desert training exercise before reporting back to our Team. The last day was a brutal ten-hour land navigation course in the scorching Niland, California, heat, and after dinner, we were all smoked, severely dehydrated, and ready for bed. But the instructors had other plans for us. They put on a last-minute twelve-mile nighttime desert death march with a full rucksack, our weapons, ammo, and other equipment.

About halfway through the course, Rob dropped out due to heat exhaustion. He'd had enough and knew he couldn't push himself any further, so he popped his strobe light for the ambulance to come find him. In all fairness, others started dropping out like New York liberals at a Trump rally, but Rob was the first. And because he had been such a jerk to everyone all the time—giving them shit for any minor infraction—the class turned on him, jumping at the chance to exploit his weakness.

He got the nickname "Disco" for lighting off his strobe and being the first to quit the ruck march. This followed him back to Team 3, where he got off to a rough start to his SEAL career. During his first platoon as a new guy, where you'd best keep your mouth shut and do as you're told, he couldn't help himself. Rob popped off his mouth to Tim, his seasoned platoon-leading petty officer (what we call an LPO in the Navy). One week later, he was sent to a disciplinary board full of senior Navy SEALs who pulled his Trident pin and sent him back to the regular Navy in disgrace.

Years later, after I had become a sniper instructor, I was taking my son Jackson to the pool to jump off the high platforms for fun when I saw Rob. He was a recycled student, back in dive phase, forced to do all of SEAL training over again five years later. I couldn't believe my eyes—and of course, I made him drop for a bunch of push-ups before Jackson and I went for an afternoon swim.

After telling Tyler this story, I said, "Nobody likes working with a talented jerk, Tyler, and Rob demonstrates this very clearly."

I could tell Tyler got the message.

His sophomore year, he made the team again, and the coach—the same one who had kicked Tyler off the team as a freshman—sent Gretchen an email about what a different kid Tyler had turned into:

Hi Gretchen,

I hope this finds you well. I know it's been a few months since we last connected, but I wanted to reach out to you regarding Tyler, and I can assure you that it's all positive!

I pulled Tyler aside tonight after the open gym had ended because I wanted to let him know that I'm so proud of him for the transformation he's been through in terms of his maturity and skillset. While his basketball skills have also reached another level, it's more important to me for an athlete to have good character over being a good player. Tyler has always had a great heart and passion but now he's clearly learned how to harness it and knows when to unleash it. Overall, I'm so happy for him and everyone has noticed his evolution in such a short time period. All the other coaches and players have acknowledged it to me or amongst themselves. Both you and Tyler deserve all the credit in the world for accepting my feedback from this past November and using it as motivation to show that he belongs in the Mountainside Basketball program. While the journey for Tyler is still ongoing, as it is for any human in life, I just wanted to ensure that you both were aware of the positive impact Tyler has had on everyone because of his determination and effort to be at his best. There's been many times throughout these open gyms where Tyler could've become upset or angry, and truthfully, I wouldn't have blamed him, but his ability to internalize any frustration and quickly move onto the next play is incredible and something that I have yet to consistently master for myself. Thank you so much for your support and understanding. I'm excited to see what the future holds for Tyler.

Best,
Coach Ryan

These are the moments you live for as a parent. It was such a pleasure watching Tyler play basketball that year and seeing how he had turned into an unselfish playmaker and a real team player who kept his cool under pressure. Boy, were his mom and I proud to get that letter from Coach Ryan!

Jackson's First Credit Card

A conversation I had with all my kids in their teens went something like this: "Look, your mom and I have been through hell for you guys to have a good life. The only thing you owe us is to reach for your dreams and know that if you stumble and fall, we'll always be here for you. You'll always have a roof over your head. But there are no free handouts." I then explained that I'd foot the bill for college but not their social life. For that, they needed to get a job, or in Jackson's case, I offered for him to run a small investment I had made in a self-storage facility in Orlando, Florida.

Jackson took to it like a fish to water, switching all the tenants to digital leases, building a website, and installing storage software to help us manage the tenants and financials. He did an excellent job, and we found ourselves with a facility that was nearly fully occupied and worth more than double what we paid for it in less than two years. We decided to sell the property, and I'd given him a small equity stake, which was $50,000 after the sale. He reinvested half and spent the rest like a drunken sailor on shore leave at some exotic port-of-call.

Then when Jackson returned to the University of St. Andrews in Scotland for his sophomore year of college, he called me up. "Dad," he said, "I'm going to get a credit card to build my credit."

"That's great," I replied. "Just make sure you pay it off every month because the high interest will eat you alive."

"Yeah, Dad, for sure."

Then what I feared would happen, happened.

A year later, I got another call.

"Dad, I'm really sorry," Jackson said this time, "but I got myself into a situation and owe $17,000-plus on my credit card, and the interest payments are going to kill me." (He's always been good at math!)

I replied, "Do you remember what we talked about?"

"Yeah, Dad, of course."

"Then not sure what you're asking me; it's yours to deal with. Oh yeah, and welcome to adulthood."

The line went silent. I could tell it was not what he had expected. Then I said, "Look, Jackson, if I bail you out of this, what lesson are you going to learn?"

"I get it, Dad."

End of conversation.

I could tell he was stressed, and I could have paid off the card, but I knew this would leave an impression on him. As a parent, you don't want your child to suffer, but you have to understand that in some cases, suffering builds strength. I knew if he learned this lesson while still in college, Jackson would become a more responsible adult with his personal finances. It pained me to see him struggling, but I knew he needed to learn this one the hard way.

How many times have we seen family members or friends who just can't seem to manage their own finances, either living paycheck to paycheck or asking to get bailed out in their adult years? This is not the fate I wanted for my kids. I wanted Jackson and his siblings to be personally independent and financially savvy, and I knew a little short-term discomfort would imprint a lasting lesson. It took him almost three years to pay for that mistake—and he actually thanked me when it was all over.

The same way I studied corporate signaling (good and bad) in business school, I knew this would send the right kind of signal to his siblings: Dad will not always be there to bail us out for our financial mistakes. Maybe that's tough love, but it's also the ordinary magic of figuring it out on your own.

Accomplishments Big and Small

These three stories are just snapshots from my kids' lives when I realized the power of ordinary magic at work. There were plenty more, and if you keep an eye out, you'll start recognizing them too. Opportunities to build confidence in our children are around every corner, through every accomplishment, whether big or small. And of course, what we see as small accomplishments for our kids may, in their eyes, be huge.

Take Madison again. A budding creator at sixteen, kids at school noticed when she started painting on her own sneakers and offered her money to paint on their Air Force 1s. My friend Maria founded and runs a boutique events empire in New York, and she had seen Madison's Instagram account, where she'd been posting photos of the sneakers she'd been modifying. Maria reached out to me one day and explained that Puma needed an in-store artist at Saks Fifth Avenue over the Christmas holiday. Would Madison be up for it? I talked it over with her and Gretchen. I saw it as an opportunity to build up her confidence, and everyone agreed.

So Maddie flew to New York, where I was living at the time, and crashed at my place in Flatiron. She rode the subway uptown alone to grind out twelve-hour shifts painting shoes for customers. By day three, she was navigating midtown like a local, head held high, and making $1,000 a day. I loved seeing her rise to the occasion and recognize her worth. That summer, she got invited to the Hamptons for another event because she'd done such a great job with the Puma in-store.

The summer after Jackson's sophomore year in high school was another masterclass in earned independence. He mapped out a plan and pitched me on a school trip to Morocco, a solo month learning Spanish in Andalucía, and then a train ride to Madrid, where he would link up for a few weeks with Dad. I could've worried myself into insomnia, but how do you say no to a young teenager who's laying down a road map for competency? He came back fluent in more than just language—he spoke the dialect of self-reliance.

The next year, Jackson wanted a taste of corporate New York, so I helped him get a two-week summer internship at a contact's recruiting firm. He rode the subway, did his internship alongside college kids, sat in real meetings, and discovered that professionalism isn't gated by age. Sure, he had to bail when the interns hit the bar for drinks after work, but the lesson landed. If you can hold your own in that arena at seventeen, the world's not as intimidating as it looks.

Tyler, meanwhile, had his sights set on Duke basketball camp at age twelve. I asked his mom if she'd sign off on the live-and-play option—solo room, daily drills, and no parents hovering. She agreed. For a week, he made every decision himself—from laundry to lights-out—and he came home taller in spirit, if not in height. (It would be a while until he had his growth spurt, but he ended up being six four as a high school senior.)

One of my favorite snapshots of T-Man is from around that time. Me and the kids were hustling through the Portland airport, back in the glory days before they replaced that legendary green-and-blue carpet. (If you've lived there, or seen *Portlandia*, you know it wasn't just a floor—it was a cult following.) We finally made it to the food court to grab a bite, but our flight to New York was still a ways off. That's when T-Man suddenly froze.

Standing just a few tables away were a bunch of his heroes, all his favorite Portland Timbers players. Tyler's eyes lit up, and he looked at me like "Dad, can you ask for an autograph?" I didn't budge. Instead, I told him, "Life's short. You want that autograph? You're old enough to go ask for it. You've got this, buddy. But you've gotta do it on your own." His siblings jumped in, his own personal hype squad, egging him on. After a minute of wrestling with his nerves, he stood up, walked over, and asked. He came back grinning, autograph in hand, confidence turned up ten notches.

Moments like that one may seem small, but they're a product of something bigger. That confidence didn't come out of nowhere. It came from years of reinforcing a family culture where stepping up was normal, where siblings rooted for each other, and where independence was expected, not feared. Sure, I could have gotten that autograph for him. But that would've stolen the real prize. The win wasn't the ink on the paper—it was the courage it took to get it.

Even our wildcards have turned into confidence jackpots. Twelve-year-old Madison once visited me in New York, and she wanted to go flying in my plane. I strapped her into my Vans RV-6 and showed her how to roll the plane inverted off the coast of Brooklyn after we did a few laps around Lady Liberty. I still remember what she said over the internal comms. "That was easy, Dad!" How many adults have the courage to try that, let alone a young girl? Another proud moment for yours truly.

Confidence isn't gifted; it's taught early, earned, and proudly worn like a warm blanket in the future. And though you'll play the most important role in helping your kids develop this sense of confidence, other adults will end up influencing it as well—whether you like it or not. Which brings me to one of the most important lessons I can share with any parent: Your kid's environment will make or break them.

Surround Your Kids with Good People

I don't care if you're Parent of the Century. You can read all the parenting books, prep organic meals, and run a damn military-style calendar of structure and values at home. But if your kid is marinating in garbage—bad friends, toxic coaches, half-ass teachers, and emotionally bankrupt adults—you're fighting a losing battle. Environment isn't just important; it's everything.

That's why I was relentless about surrounding my kids with people who inspired them: mentors, coaches, and trusted friends.

Whether it was picking the right school or just steering them toward high-caliber peers, I treated it like I was building a SEAL platoon for a mission. No weak links. No energy vampires.

If our kids are placed in the right environments, around people who do hard things, they'll start to believe they can do hard things too. The Center on the Developing Child at Harvard University published a working paper titled "Place Matters: The Environment We Create Shapes the Foundations of Healthy Development." It emphasizes that the environments where children live, grow, play, and learn—encompassing both physical surroundings and social relationships—profoundly influence their development. Children raised in safe, supportive, and stimulating environments are more likely to thrive, while those in adverse settings may encounter more challenges that hinder their growth.

Crafting a positive environment is like setting the stage for your child's success, providing them with the tools and support they need to flourish. It's about the people, the experiences, and the culture that envelop your child daily. I think the winning formula is to provide a great, loving environment and manufacture adversity for our children to make their roots grow strong. Remember, most of us no longer have the village to fall back on, so it's up to us to build one. Your village, and the environment surrounding it, is of massive importance.

Want a sneak peek at your kids' trajectory? Don't check their grades; check their group chat. You can hire tutors, set curfews, and read all the parenting blogs in the universe, but if your kid is surrounded by a pack of underachievers or worse, that gravitational pull is going to drag them down. "Show me your friends, and I'll show you your future" isn't just a catchy line—it's a tactical truth.

Environment is also stronger than willpower. Drop a monk in Vegas for a year with half a million dollars and see how that plays out. The same applies to your child. I don't care how "good" they are; if their peer group, coach, teacher, or school culture is toxic, they will not rise above it. Hoping they will is lazy parenting dressed up as optimism. Sometimes the only solution is to change the damn pond: different school, different coach, different zip code. I know that might sound extreme, but so is losing your kid to mediocrity, or something more insidious, because you were too afraid to make a bold move.

Still not convinced? Ask that guy named Darwin how important your surroundings are. Adaptation doesn't happen in a vacuum; it happens in response to the environment. The stronger, healthier, and more stimulating the ecosystem, the more potential your kid has to evolve and thrive. This isn't theory—it's survival.

Living in New York through my kids' middle and high school years gave me an edge. Manhattan is a pressure cooker of ambition, creativity, and execution. I *love* this about New York, and few cities come close to Manhattan in this regard. I was surrounded by an eclectic group of friends: founders, artists, financiers, authors, coders, dancers, musicians, stylists, and executives. Every chance I got, I'd bring one of my kids along to a dinner, an important meeting, or an event if I thought it would leave a mark.

This was intentional. I wasn't just introducing them to cool people; I was curating their exposure to high-functioning, positive adult role models, people who were doing their thing and doing it well. This was especially important for Madison. From the time she was a teenager, she had that fire; you could tell she was going to carve out her own path. So I made sure she had a front-row seat to badass girl bosses every chance I got.

She met Sally Richardson, the legendary publisher at St. Martin's Press at the time; Alyssa, my former agent at WME, who moves in a world full of sharks and never flinches; and, of course, Maria, who got Maddie the Puma gig. Then there was Sally Lyndley, a fashion stylist working with Victoria Beckham and *Love* magazine, and Sarah, the executive at iHeart Media who commands boardrooms like a four-star general. Madison didn't have to imagine what a successful woman looked like; she got to meet her and ask questions. These were future archetypes.

Don't underestimate the impact other positive adults can have on your kids. As a parent, your voice can start to sound like background static—especially to a teenager who's heard you give the same pep talk a hundred times. Then out of nowhere, when someone else says the exact same thing you've been preaching for years, they'll take it as gospel.

Case in point: When my son Tyler met my buddy Brent Burns, who plays professional hockey, Brent shook his hand and said, "Hey kid, you've got a solid handshake." That's it—seven words. For the next week, Tyler walked around like John Wayne, chest out, handshake ready for anyone within reach. That's the power of letting your kids cross paths with positive, inspiring people.

Here's the thing: You don't have to be friends with professional athletes, corporate executives, successful creatives, or Navy SEALs. Your "village" might already be full of people who can make a lasting impression: a teacher who believes in them, a neighbor who runs a small business, a coach who pushes them just hard enough, a family friend who's mastered a craft or trade. Even a retired neighbor with a killer vegetable garden can plant seeds in more ways than one.

Mentors

Which brings me to mentors, like the one I found in Bill Magee. Mentors for your kids won't just appear by magic, ordinary or otherwise—you've got to make it happen. Ask friends. Reach out to people you trust and respect. Ask them, "Would you be willing to take my kid under your wing a bit? Share your story? Give them a sense of what's possible?" Most folks will be flattered you asked, and you'd be surprised how often they'll say yes.

Kids with mentors are more likely to succeed in school, avoid risky behaviors, and report higher self-esteem. A large-scale study by psychologist Jean E. Rhodes and researcher David L. DuBois found that mentored youth had stronger academic performance and better emotional well-being compared to their peers without mentors. The presence of even one trusted adult outside the family can literally change the trajectory of a child's life.

I've seen this play out in my own world. For example, the new introductory class I'd developed on mental management for snipers included an incentive for the instructors to put maximum effort into the students. We did this using a mentorship program that created accountability and aligned incentives for all parties. We'd assign four students (two sniper pairs) to each instructor. This ensured I got the most out of my instructors—you didn't want to be the one whose students were failing! My guys put in a ton of extra hours to ensure their students understood the course material and were performing at the highest level.

Once I left the SEALs, I found incredible mentors through the Young Presidents' Organization (YPO), an international leadership community, which challenged me, called me on my blind spots, and showed me how to navigate life after the SEAL Teams. Those relationships weren't accidents; they were built intentionally. And that's the same opportunity we can create for our kids.

That's why, after each of my kids finished high school, I matched them with a mentor from my own network: someone who could challenge them, guide them, and give them a different perspective. You can do the same in your world. The mentors are out there. All you have to do is ask.

My kids still laugh about how, in New York, they got to hang out with "Dad's friends," from artists to firemen to a guy who made the best bagels in the East Village. They didn't care about background; they just thought it was cool that grown-ups outside our family wanted to spend time with them. What they may not have realized then, however, is that they were learning life lessons they'd carry forward with them into all their endeavors.

The Heart of Confidence

Today, my kids don't fear failing or making mistakes. They know these are simply part of life, and they have learned this fact through their own experiences and those of mine I've shared with them. When they get knocked down, they get back up with intention—and as a parent, this is a wonderful thing to see.

Falling isn't failure. Not trying in the first place or staying down when knocked over is. The greatest gift we can give our children isn't a life free of struggle; it's the courage to confront struggle and the faith that they will rise stronger because of it. That's the ordinary magic we need to expose them to. I know how tempting it is to protect them from every fall, to smooth every bump in the road. I've been there, wanting to shield Madison from disappointment or rush in when things got hard on the ranch for the boys. But if I were to have done that, I would have robbed them of the chance to discover something far more precious than comfort: their own strength.

The Minnesota kids researched by Dr. Masten—those who faced hardship and came out confident—didn't have superpowers. They had ordinary magic, the kind that lives in scraped knees, failed tests, and "not yet" moments. They had parents who believed in them enough to let them try, fail, and try again. And that belief became the fire that lit their way forward.

When your child stumbles, when their dreams feel just out of reach, don't fix the problem for them. Stand beside them. Hold their hand. Remind them that falling isn't failing—it's part of becoming. In those moments of struggle, they're not just learning how to get back up. They're learning who they are and how the real world works outside of the parental biosphere.

And that, my friend, is the heart of confidence. Not perfection. Not the easy way out. But the fierce, unshakable knowledge that no matter what life throws their way, they have what it takes to rise. This is the legacy we give our children. The quiet, powerful, ordinary magic of resilience. The courage to navigate the world with their heads held high. The gift of knowing they are enough, just as they are and just as they will become.

Let's give them that gift. Let's trust them with the hard parts and watch them soar.

Field Note: Confidence Is Earned

- Let them carry weight early. Start small—swim lessons, bikes, chores—and stack skills over time so confidence becomes muscle memory.
- Make the village intentional. Surround them with mentors, coaches, and peers who set the bar high and show them what's possible.
- Stand back, stay close. Let them own the task, win or lose, but be there to help them process and rise after they fall.

Family Challenge: This month, arrange one intentional meet-up with someone you trust to inspire your child.

Advice from Madison: *Hearing at a young age that even parents made mistakes, weren't good at things right away, and embarrassed themselves makes kids more comfortable with their own failure.*

Chapter Checklist

- **Let Them Fail Without a Net (Sometimes).** Don't race in to fix every misstep. Let them fall, reflect, and get back up. That's how confidence is born.
- **Assign Real Responsibility Early.** Give them meaningful tasks that matter, whether managing a younger sibling for an afternoon, making dinner for the family, or running a weekend errand.
- **Create a Family Culture of Earning, Not Entitlement.** Whether it's a purple belt or a trip abroad, make them work for it. Confidence skyrockets when achievement is earned, not handed out.
- **Turn Setbacks into Strategy Sessions.** Normalize talking through what went wrong. Whether it's a failed test or a dropped sports team, ask them, "What would you do differently next time?"
- **Model Resilience with Real-Life Examples.** Share your own failures and what you learned from them. Vulnerability builds trust and shows your kids that even heroes stumble.
- **Say Yes to Ordinary Magic Moments.** Give them space to lead. Have them plan a family hike, run a garage sale, or even negotiate their allowance. Ordinary moments create extraordinary growth.
- **Encourage Entrepreneurial Spirit.** Got a kid who paints shoes, like Madison? Fan that spark. Let them hustle and learn the ropes of business, confidence, and independence all in one go.
- **Link Environment to Expectations.** Keep them surrounded by mentors, coaches, and peers who challenge and uplift them. Their peer group can do more for their competence than any lecture ever will.
- **Let Consequences Teach When Words Can't.** A $17,000 credit card bill like Jackson's? Painful, but unforgettable. Don't rob them of a lesson just because it's hard to watch.
- **Celebrate Effort, Not Just Results.** Recognize the grit it took to try, to persist, to bounce back from failure. That's how you build confidence for the long haul.

3

Disciplining with Love

Power is of two kinds. One is obtained by the fear of punishment and the other by acts of love. Power based on love is a thousand times more effective and permanent than the one derived from fear of punishment.

—MAHATMA GANDHI

When it comes to parenting, I truly believe in Gandhi's wisdom—great parents always lead with love. While there are times when discipline is necessary, our primary job as parents is to ensure all other options are exhausted before pulling that lever. And there's a *big* difference between discipline and punishment. Discipline teaches. Punishment penalizes and builds fear. As parents, we need to recognize this difference.

In the SEAL Teams, we have various forms of discipline to address mistakes. I can assure you that when I was disciplined as a new SEAL—and believe me, it happened more often than I'd like to admit—it was always crystal clear as to why. We must bring this same type of clarity to parenting. Too often, I see parents quick to dish out punishments to confused children. The result? Further confusion, followed by resentment and, as most research confirms, long-term harm. A 2016 meta-analysis of seventy-five studies published in the *Journal of Family Psychology* found that corporal punishment was consistently linked to increased aggression, antisocial behavior, and mental health struggles later in life. On the other hand, studies from the American Academy of Pediatrics show that positive discipline strategies—like clear boundaries and consistent consequences—are far more effective in teaching kids self-control and empathy. Punishment may stop a behavior in the moment, but discipline that teaches and guides with love shapes character for life.

It's a lot like raising a puppy. Anyone who's ever tried to train one knows that harsh punishment does not work—it just creates fear and confusion for the poor pup. The monks of New Skete, a monastic community in upstate New York famous for raising and training German shepherds, built their entire philosophy around this idea. Their dogs aren't obedient because they're scared; they're obedient because they've been guided with love, consistency, and incentive-based rewards. The monks prove that discipline, done right, builds trust and confidence, not fear.

Parenting works the same way. Our kids aren't projects to be broken down into compliance—they're souls to be shaped. And just as a puppy learns best through gentle correction and steady encouragement, children thrive when the structure we provide is rooted in love, clarity, and consistency.

Here's a little-known fact: After 90 percent of SEALs wash out in selection, about 10 percent of the remaining SEALs who make it through initial training still wash out at the Team level. Most people simply can't perform the required skills effectively under such intense physical and intellectual pressure, including the cognitive ability to shoot, move, and communicate in the moment. This harsh reality drives our saying, "Earn your Trident every day." It's all about consistent standards.

When I was in close-quarters combat shooting school at a remote facility in Tennessee, we trained over eight hours a day for two weeks in hostage rescue scenarios, navigating complex house mazes under life-or-death conditions. Our sixteen-man SEAL platoon would stack at the main entrance, waiting for the go signal to flow through the building. Boom! The door would blow open. One man right, one left, one right, one left, shots ringing out, as we cleared room after room until the house was secure.

We'd breach locked doors with explosives and deploy stun grenades where needed, flowing through the house like a high-speed train, shooting hostile targets and protecting hostages. To elevate the stakes, we used live ammunition. When firing real bullets inches away from your teammates, you can't miss or "drop" a round. Every action is recorded on video. There's no escaping the feedback.

Shoot a hostage once or twice, and you'd get counseled with an immediate review of the video footage. You'd then be sent outside to pull a massive tractor tire hundreds of yards in full gear while your SEAL platoon took a water break and watched, hoping they weren't next. If you missed your shots? Same consequence. A third mistake meant facing a disciplinary review board of senior SEALs who would determine whether to recycle you to another SEAL platoon or return you to regular Navy service.

When I missed a shot for the first time, I was given the opportunity to explain what went wrong before watching the video recording and receiving feedback. Crucially, I felt heard before taking my consequence. And let me tell you, dragging that enormous tractor tire with a thick, gym-like climbing rope while wearing full combat gear is excruciating, especially with your peers watching. It was a hard lesson, but I only had to pull that tire once—I tightened up my performance immediately.

Later, as a sniper instructor, if a student missed an important shot without good reason, we'd make them run three miles in full gear carrying their rifle to drive home a critical message: "Hit your target the first time, every time." The problem with poor leadership, whether in the military or parenting, is that people are often punished without understanding why. Good parenting, like good leadership, requires clear communication about expectations and reasons behind consequences. It also requires you to set your own consistent standards early on—as to what is and is not an acceptable form of discipline.

A New Approach

Discipline in my house growing up came in one flavor—leather. It was swift, firm, and for that generation, considered normal. My dad worked construction from sunup to sundown, his hands calloused and his arms and face sun-beaten from long days on the job. He carried that same toughness home. He wasn't cruel—just doing what he thought a good father did: turn a boy into a man, tough enough to take on the world. That's what his father taught him, and probably what his father taught before that.

As a kid, I didn't always understand it. Some moments stayed with me—not just the ones you could see, but the kind that quietly shape how a kid learns about strength, control, and love. Looking back now, I don't feel anger; I feel gratitude mixed with perspective. My dad's lessons were born from hard work and survival. When I became a father, I realized that strength can be built another way, through kindness, patience, leading by example, and the steady work of building kids up, not breaking them down.

Still, I wasn't exactly an easy kid to raise. My mom, God bless her, only reported my offenses if they were really bad, and there were plenty. I had a special talent for pushing her RPMs into the red from an early age. In fact, I was such a handful that she once called child protective services on herself because she was losing it with my behavior.

When the officer got there, as the story goes, I turned into a perfect angel, because, of course, I suddenly had someone new to play with. The lady looked at my mom like she was out of her mind. "What a sweet little boy," she said. My mom just stood there in shock as the door closed behind her.

Eventually she learned how to harness my energy with skiing and other physical activities. I'm pretty sure I would have been diagnosed with ADHD, but back then, doctors recommended activity over medication. I eventually got better with age, but I was still a handful until I wasn't. So as my dad walked through the door on a typical evening of me pushing my mom to her limits, she'd lay out my rap sheet of the day. "Broke a window after I told him to stop throwing the ball at the house. Blew up the bathroom pipes with fireworks at school. Made fun of his sister until she cried," she'd say like a court clerk. And like in a Russian courthouse, I knew the verdict before the case even started.

"Get upstairs, now," my father would growl.

It was swift, it was painful, and it left marks—not just the welts, but the kind that sink deep into how a kid learns to view authority, control, and fear. I'm not here to throw my dad under the bus; I love him, and I know he was doing what he thought best. That was how he grew up. His father did the same to him, and it's what every man on my block in the late '80s probably did to their kids too.

When I was maybe seven or eight, I told a lie, nothing major, but enough to set him off. He grabbed a bar of Irish Spring and shoved it in my mouth for what felt like an hour. My whole mouth swelled up. I looked like I'd lost a boxing match, my lips puffed out like a fish pulled up too fast from deep water. It burned, it stung, and it stuck with me, not just the taste, but the lesson underneath it. I still can't stand the smell of that soap! That moment became a line in the sand for me, even if I didn't know it yet.

But I wanted to break the kind of generational trauma that comes with a blue-collar-work-ethic-fueled ass whooping. So when Gretchen and I had Jackson, we made a pact. No hitting. Not even a little. Not in anger, not in frustration, not because "That's just how it's done." I didn't want my kids to fear my shadow in the doorway. I wanted them to respect me, not flinch when I raised my voice. Gretchen, tough as she is, was even more adamant. We agreed: no violence in discipline. Not because we were trying to raise soft kids, but because we knew there was a harder path, a better one.

Turns out, we weren't just going on our gut.

Case Study: Physical Punishment and Child Development

A 2016 meta-analysis by researchers Elizabeth Gershoff and Andrew Grogan-Kaylor, which looked at over 160,000 kids, found that spanking and physical punishment didn't make children better behaved—it made them worse. More aggressive. More defiant. More likely to develop mental health issues. The American Academy of Pediatrics backed this finding up in 2018, flat-out stating that hitting your kid, even once, is not only ineffective; it's harmful. All you're doing is wiring your children for more aggression and teaching them to respond to conflict with force. By hitting—or screaming at—your kids, they learn to fear pain and obey power, not build judgment, self-respect, or emotional control.

Think about it for a moment and ask yourself this question: "Is this how problems are solved in the workplace?" You know the answer.

Instead of punishment, researchers advocate for discipline that actually works: clear expectations, time-outs, and earned consequences—real accountability without the trauma. By being smart and deliberate, you raise kids who think instead of flinch. In our house, instead of spankings, we doled out push-ups or wall sits.

Don't lose the attitude? Lose the screen time.

Break trust? Goodbye allowance.

Gretchen and I settled on push-ups and taking privileges away as our main source of discipline because we wanted our kids to feel discomfort, but the right kind—the kind that teaches resilience and accountability without breaking their spirit. Our rule was that if there was an offense committed, they would have to give us one push-up for every year of age or a wall sit for one minute.

With push-ups, I'd say in my SEAL instructor voice, "They don't count unless you count!" as they started to push 'em out. My kids still laugh about this, and they admitted to me when they were older that it was more embarrassing having to do their push-ups in front of an audience than the actual act itself. Good to know!

Make no mistake: Our house had discipline. But it was the kind that builds a backbone, not bruises. And it worked. Push a kid into physical exertion instead of emotional shame, and you get a human being who learns that actions have consequences. That's the difference between control and leadership. And that's the mold we chose to break.

Discipline bad behavior with clear consequences, communicate why, and don't forget to reward good behavior—it's that simple. This last point is important: Rewarding good behavior reinforces that doing good brings good things. We rewarded the kids for being polite in public, telling an important truth, being brave, performing a good deed, getting good grades in school, and doing well in sports. We always emphasized more reward for intellectual achievement over sports, but that was our choice. Positive reinforcement rewards came in the form of cold hard cash via Venmo, dinner of their choice, a new cell phone, a special trip, or a toy or bike they really wanted. By both disciplining bad behavior and rewarding good behavior, you can help condition your kids to behave and conduct themselves in a positive way.

Also, I can't emphasize this enough: You have to follow through.

Don't Be a Pushover

Lack the courage to stick to your guns and your kids will come to know you as a pushover. For example, Gretchen was driving the kids to school one day, and she was yelling at them to stop their bickering in the back of our Honda Odyssey, which I nicknamed the "urban assault vehicle." She said something like "If you don't stop arguing, you'll be grounded." Then Gretchen overheard Madison say to Tyler, "Don't worry, she'll just forget." That made a big impression on her, and on me, reinforcing the importance of follow-through for us both.

As a result, we made sure to stick to our guns as much as possible. One time, I took the kids to SeaWorld in San Diego for the day by myself, giving Gretchen a break and getting the chance for some dad time with the kids. As they were fighting and arguing, I said, "Guys, quiet down or I'll turn around and no SeaWorld." It was quiet for a few minutes, then they started back in on each other. I turned off at the next exit, and the whole car went dead silent.

"Dad, what's going on?" Madison asked.

"I told you guys what would happen. We're going home."

If Hans Zimmer were to score a kids-crying scene, cue the music as my Toyota Tacoma became an amphitheater of tears and begs for mercy. Two weeks later, I took them back, and it was like I had three nuns riding with me. My kids had learned that Dad wasn't messing around.

The good news is, you typically only have to do this once or twice before they understand that you're serious, then it's easy to get them in line when you need to by laying out a real consequence. Don't make threats you don't want to follow through on. If we had purchased tickets to Hawai'i and were driving to the airport, I would not say we were going to cancel the trip, because it would be super expensive and impractical. Only threaten them with what's reasonable and what you're willing to enforce.

When Discipline Is the Wrong Option

Even with the right kind of discipline, sometimes you still have to pump the brakes. Let me share a time when this played out for Gretchen and me. Our youngest son, Tyler, the James Dean of our family, had been struggling to maintain focus in class and was diagnosed with ADHD at the beginning of seventh grade. T-Man is a quiet, moody, deep thinker with a natural charisma that draws people to him. Everyone loves him. But he has also been our most challenging child to parent, a bit like taming a wild stallion at times.

(My mother, Lynn, says he's my karmic payback for the hell I put her through as a teenager, and she's probably right.)

After his ADHD diagnosis, Gretchen and I committed to supporting his condition without prescription medication. We were surprised at how quickly doctors suggested pills for an energetic teenage boy navigating puberty. Instead, we enrolled him in meditation classes and ensured he stayed active in sports. We saw immediate improvements in his attitude and ability to pay attention, both at home and at school, until I received this text from his mom:

"Tyler was suspended from school. Can you talk?"

"Right away," I messaged back.

When something like this happened, it became my primary focus. I'd clear my entire schedule, unlike some parents who consistently prioritize work over family. I've witnessed this repeatedly in my business network: good people who love their children but don't place them on equal footing with their careers. It's hard, I get it—and I don't judge—but you have to consider the repercussions as well. Your children eventually understand whether they're a genuine priority in your life, and as a parent, you'll live with the consequences of that mindset. The rewards of making kids a priority can be profound too. After my son Jackson graduated from the University of St. Andrews in 2024, he hugged me and said, "Well . . . I kind of won the dad lottery." These are the moments I treasure most. I've always believed my children should see that they're a priority for both their mother and me, and I believe that's helped all of us along the way, including in times like these.

So when I called Gretchen, I learned that Tyler had been suspended for ordering pizza to his classroom via Uber Eats. In a scene out of *Fast Times at Ridgemont High*, the teacher confiscated the pizza, told Tyler food delivery wasn't allowed in class, and then ate it. Tyler's response the next day? He thought he'd found a clever work-around by sending not one but *twenty* pizzas to the principal's office instead. This went over about as well as you'd imagine. T-Man was promptly suspended.

Gretchen and I were extremely upset, especially when we learned Tyler had also been talking back to his teacher. But we had no idea what was really driving this behavior. Our first instinct was punitive. We considered confiscating his cell phone, restricting activities with friends, and our classic physical consequence at that point—push-ups.

However, sometimes situations aren't as straightforward as they initially appear. The real question was, Why was Tyler acting out when we thought we had gotten him to a good place? After Gretchen and I traded various consequence ideas, I suggested consulting the psychologist who had helped us through our divorce. Perhaps she could advise us on the most effective approach.

We were about to receive a profound parenting lesson.

Getting to the Root Cause

Later that week, we spoke with Dr. Baker in California. She explained that our priority should be uncovering the root of Tyler's behavioral issues by talking to him just as we would to an adult.

"Just ask him why he did it," she advised.

The suggestion sounded almost too simple, so straightforward that I felt foolish for not thinking of it myself. But this exemplifies a major parenting insight: Often, we let fear guide us to discipline or punishment without truly understanding why our children act out. We had nearly made a serious error, but Dr. Baker helped us navigate away from potential disaster. Tyler's older siblings had been relatively easy through their teenage years; both were naturally academic and well-behaved. By comparison, Tyler's behavior seemed so disproportionate that we panicked and prepared to impose every consequence imaginable.

"Boys have it tough from ages twelve to sixteen with all their hormones, especially these days," Dr. Baker explained in her reassuring voice. "It's very complicated for young boys. If you don't identify the source of his behavior and instead punish him blindly, you'll only push him further away, causing the situation to deteriorate further."

Dr. Baker gave us our homework, and I flew to Portland to spend one of my dad-and-kid one-on-one weeks with Tyler. Though we'd typically go on an adventure together, in this case my goal was to visit him at home and facilitate deeper conversations about his future. Before my trip, Gretchen agreed to begin exploring the why behind Tyler's actions with him. What we discovered together was shocking.

We learned that Tyler's homeroom teacher had repeatedly berated him in front of the entire class, accusing him of being spoiled and, in full view of his peers, labeling him as such. I was stunned. As a chief petty officer, I learned early that effective leaders never criticize publicly. You praise in public and provide constructive feedback in private. A few days before my flight to Oregon, Gretchen called with more information. Over the previous three months, Tyler's relationship with his homeroom teacher had deteriorated dramatically, and he was pushing back the only way he knew how—pizza deliveries.

Even more concerning, Gretchen discovered this teacher had received five parental complaints for treating students like she did Tyler in the past year alone. *Five!* Gretchen spoke with the school principal, who explained that the district was contending with a severe shortage of qualified teachers. While he acknowledged the classroom situation was "unfortunate," all he could do was speak to the teacher again. Staffing limitations tied his hands.

We both spoke with T-Man, assured him we were on his side, and stated our commitment to finding a solution together. His visible relief told us everything. What began as a search for the appropriate consequence for his behavior transformed into a mission to restore Tyler to a positive learning environment.

Though we had completed much of the groundwork before my Oregon trip, when I got there, I still had valuable conversations with Tyler about navigating difficult authority figures. I shared my own experiences with challenging teachers and bosses, explaining how these had ultimately become growth opportunities for me. Tyler started coming around, especially when he realized his mom and I had his back.

The outcome? Rather than punishing a child who was acting out, we took a different, proactive approach. Having mapped the situation, gathered the information, and aligned on outcomes, the proportional response was clear. We arranged an independent study for Tyler for the remainder of the seventh and all of the eighth grade. This removed him from a toxic environment and provided one in which he could thrive and succeed. Following that shift, Tyler made an excellent transition to high school and held a 3.0–3.5 GPA throughout. After graduation, he was off to the University of Oregon. Go Ducks, go T-Man!

This experience reinforced a key parenting principle: Always understand the purpose or "why" behind a behavior before deciding on its consequences. Ensure both you and your child fully understand the situation before implementing discipline. Otherwise, you risk making a difficult situation worse while pushing your children away. Listening and understanding must precede any disciplinary action with your children. Consider this the next time you rush to sentencing without a proper investigation. And no matter the findings, remember, there is such a thing as overdisciplining.

"Operation Weed" and Overdisciplining

Our first experience with drugs in the house was when Jackson was a junior in high school, Madison was a freshman, and Tyler was on home study, with a ringside seat to what was about to unfold. Jackson had recently broken up with his first serious girlfriend in high school, but they remained on as good of terms as you can at that age. She ended up moving a few counties away to live with family, but before she left, she gave Jackson a little parting gift—a bag of weed she didn't want to risk taking with her.

Jackson, being a highly emotionally intelligent seventeen-year-old and a budding entrepreneur, came up with a plan to turn teenage heartbreak into a little extra spending cash. Knowing his sister Madison and her friends were way cooler than he was, he asked her if she could find a buyer for this "product" that had come his way. She reluctantly agreed and tucked the bag of weed under her bed.

Before I go any further, you have to understand something about the kids' mother—Gretchen is an absolute clean freak. If she were ever in the military, she would have earned the respect of the most hardened drill instructors for her cleanliness and attention to detail. I have always admired this about her, because I'm obsessive when it comes to keeping a tidy space. But this fastidiousness would ultimately be the downfall of "Operation Weed."

During a routine cleaning inspection, Gretchen found the contraband and rightfully went from calm mom to angry momma bear in half a second. I got a phone call briefing me on the situation, and we agreed I would stand by while she investigated further.

Selling drugs? How could my little Maddie get caught up in this?

Tyler had overheard his mom talking to me, and being a good, loyal sibling (Madison and Tyler have always been close), he tipped her off at school. Years later, I heard their side of the story, and I think Tyler's text message to Madison read something like "Mom found your pot, you might not want to come home, ever."

Madison has never been one to back down, and after she heard from Tyler, I think she texted and then phoned her mom to try to explain. Gretchen, at this point, knew Madison had been tipped off by her younger brother and wasn't happy about it at all because she wanted to spring it on Madison when she got home.

Surprise ruined: Thank you, Tyler.

Madison got home after school and immediately explained the whole story through tears, probably wondering how she let her older brother get her into such a mess. When Gretchen filled me in that Jackson was the mastermind behind "Operation Weed," I was floored—he was the last person we expected. Both Madison and Jackson were extremely self-driven academics with perfect GPAs, speech and debate team champions, and generally straight-laced, high-achieving kids. At the time, Jackson had just been named an All-American for his speech and debate accomplishments, and as a junior, he was already looking at applying to some top schools. How someone so smart could put all this hard work at risk with some half-baked plan to sell pot blew our minds.

The reality was, and remains, that selling drugs in school is a pretty fucking bad idea. Especially looking at the potential consequences if they were caught by the school or police.

Not good!

When the mom gavel fell, it looked like this:

- **Tyler.** Grounded, no phone after school for two weeks for being a snitch.
- **Madison.** Grounded, no phone after school for two weeks for getting involved with the intent to sell.
- **Jackson.** Grounded, no phone after school for two weeks, and no junior prom for being the mastermind behind Operation Weed.

I expressed my opinion against not allowing Jackson to go to junior prom; it's not something that comes around twice—unless you're that forever high schooler played by Matthew McConaughey in *Dazed and Confused*—but Gretchen was steadfast. She felt this would send a serious message to Jackson's siblings, who were quite shaken at this point. Admittedly, I felt a bit bad for Tyler because I didn't see much harm in him trying to warn his sister, but I had to choose my battles. Ultimately, I sided with Gretchen, because that's what a good co-parent does. Little did Gretchen and I know that we were about to learn a lesson of our own.

Jackson had no intention of missing his junior prom. He hatched a prom night breakout that would rival Steve McQueen's *The Great*

Escape, a movie about Allied prisoners escaping a Nazi POW camp during WWII. (If you haven't seen this, put it on your watch list.) His plan, similar to McQueen's, ended with his stepdad giving chase in his truck after Jackson's buddies, who had sped around the block to snatch him after he had tunneled out of the backyard. And like McQueen, Jackson successfully evaded capture when pursued.

When Gretchen went to his room, she found a letter addressed to her sitting on the foot of his bed:

Dear Mom,

I left to go to the prom. A friend of mine picked me up and agreed to drop me off right after. Also, Scout will be bringing my things from Outdoor School to Prom so you won't have to pick them up.

I will be back by 11:30 and if not I will call/text you with one of my friends phone to ensure that you know that I am safe.

It astounds me that this year will be my eighteenth birthday. I could never tell you how lucky I feel to have had you with me every step of the way, Mom. I remember the swings in the park in San Diego, that dang Spanish school that you and Dad made me go to that totally has given me a leg up now, crying with you in my bedroom when you had to explain to me that you were getting a divorce and when we both cried but then laughed and hugged each other because snot was dripping out of my nose, the long hours you used to be away as a single mom working and dealing with Honey and Captain to give us a great childhood, the fact that you never forgot to pick me up besides that one time when Tall Grandpa had just gotten in town and then you sped over to get me, getting to go on long walks with you in the snow to just talk about life, and getting to have a sushi dinner with you for my birthday after so many years. You may not see it, but I get so emotional every time I have to think about the fact that I am leaving so soon. But every day I try to be positive and hug you and tell you how much I love you to try to show you how much all of your sacrifice really means to me. I love you so much, and I just hope that this next year can be the best yet.

However, I am going against what you told me, and I am sorry. I will be home and accept all of the consequences, and I just want to stay honest with you, especially now. My greatest fear is that you can't protect Madison and Tyler from high school, but you can be there for them with your decades of advice to help them when they do mess up, just like I have. I am scared that if their honesty is punished or dismissed with suspicion, they will only hide things from you and lie when they need your help the most. I will acknowledge that I am just a 17-year-old who hasn't raised five children, but I just want to help.

You asked me what I wanted for my birthday, and maybe it is too much, but forgiveness for this Prom would be one of two things I would want. Secondly, I just want to wake up and give you a hug to hopefully get one step closer to showing you how much I have cherished the time I have been able to spend with you.

I love you, Mom, I really mean it. See you soon,
Jackson

Gretchen called me crying to explain what had happened. I got choked up as she read the letter, and I struggled to talk through my own tears. After a few minutes had passed, we both realized we had gone too far. And when you have taken it too far as a parent, sometimes you have to swallow your pride and admit it. This is especially true as your kids turn into young adults. Gretchen and I ultimately did this with Jackson.

We also both ended up appreciating the circumstances and were glad he went to his junior prom, because when he graduated from high school a year later, it was during the pandemic. They didn't have a senior prom, and their graduation ceremony was just a masked-up drive-through with a "live" Zoom link so family could watch.

Jackson would come to live with me in Puerto Rico for his first semester at the University of St. Andrews, because he didn't feel like living in isolation, attending classes remotely from a tiny dorm room in Scotland. These six months would be some of the best in my life, and it brought us much closer together. He spent the day doing his studies while I wrote or worked through the business issues I was facing during COVID. Then we'd meet in the late afternoon and check the surf, and if it was good, we'd ride our bikes down to my friend Dennis's place, where I stored my boards, and grab a surf session.

If the surf wasn't great, Jackson would give me a chess lesson. I'd taught him the basics when he was young, but he got really into chess in high school and became quite good. (I think he's over 2000 on Lichess, and he helped me get from 1000 to 1600—it goes to show you can continue learning from your kids throughout life!) After I'd cooked dinner and given him some cooking tips, we'd convene on my roof-deck in Old San Juan under the swaying palms and tropical sky for movie night in the two hammocks I'd purchased for this specific reason.

I still have a copy of Jackson's letter, and it hits like a .50 cal sniper round to the chest every time I read it. It reminds me that parenting isn't a game of control; it's a game of compromising leadership. You don't win by dominating; you win by building trust with your kids, even when they break the rules—especially when they break the rules. Gretchen and I had to eat our slice of humble pie the night of Jackson's junior prom. But that's what it took to grow with Jackson, not just raise him.

The irony? That same kid we almost grounded into the Stone Age now runs a start-up with his best friend, Scout, the one who helped break him out of the house to attend prom. Ride or die!

Lead with Love

Watching Jackson thrive reminds me that this whole parenting thing isn't about raising rule-followers—it's about forging leaders who know when to stand up, even if it means pissing off command. We are never going to be perfect parents, but if we catch ourselves, we can always make things better. For example, one summer, when Tyler was seventeen, he and his siblings were visiting me. While he and Maddie were horsing around, he somehow managed to break the sink in my guest bathroom.

I'd been in contractor hell for months with that damn sink, making change after change, and had finally gotten it right. Then . . . CRASH! Broken. My blood pressure spiked instantly; my face turned red with rage. Without even asking what happened, I snapped. I lit into Tyler hard, right there in front of his siblings. And Tyler, being six foot three, full of fire, and seventeen, shot back with something along the lines of "I'm no bitch."

Oh, hell no.

That's when I caught myself. I literally had a flashback to me and my father right before he threw me off the family boat in Tahiti—I didn't want to repeat that with my son. So I pulled him aside, away from his brother and sister. Once we cooled down, he explained what had happened. I realized I'd come in hot, overreacting, and I apologized. We ended it with a hug. The truth is, I could always fix that sink. What mattered was repairing him.

Here's where I went wrong: I let my emotions get the best of me and the situation. I embarrassed him in front of his siblings when I should've handled it privately. I'd forgotten the lesson I'd learned in the Navy years earlier: Praise in public, discipline in private. Kids are no different than SEALs in that way.

Parenting isn't about getting it right every time. It's about catching yourself when you don't and owning it. That's real strength. And when you show your kids you're human enough to admit you blew it, their respect for you doesn't shrink; it grows.

Don't just lay down rules. Lead with love so your kids know where the guardrails are, with clarity so they understand the why, and with humility so they see you're still learning too. Sinks can be fixed. Rules can be adjusted. What sticks in their memory is the behavior you model for them: a parent who owns their mistakes, course-corrects, and keeps moving forward. That's the kind of discipline that doesn't just shape behavior; it shapes character.

Field Note: Discipline with Love and Empathy

- Teach, don't punish. Correct the behavior, keep the relationship.
- Explain the why. Clear boundary + clear reason = better buy-in.
- Let consequences teach. Make them natural, proportionate, and owned by your children.

Family Challenge: The next time one of the kids breaks a rule, ask them, "What do you think is a fair fix?" then hold them to it.

Advice from Tyler: *Looking back, the boundaries that frustrated me most ended up shaping me the most. I didn't see it then, but every time my parents followed through, they were showing me what love with structure looks like. Kids remember that kind of love, even when they act like they don't.*

Chapter Checklist

- **Develop a Plan to Discipline the Bad Behavior and Reward the Good.** Make sure both parents are in agreement and always on the same page, or your kids will learn to divide and conquer, playing Mom against Dad. Always stand firm as a parental team, or it sends the wrong signal.
- **Don't Make Threats You Don't Want to Enforce.** Is this something you are prepared to follow through on, or should you rethink and choose something else?
- **Assess Your State.** What is your current mood? If you've had a challenging day, recognize how this might affect your interaction with your child. Consider whether you need a cooling-off period.
- **Assess Your Child's State.** What is your child's emotional condition? They may not be in the right mindset to receive feedback effectively.
- **Listen First.** Ask your child to thoroughly explain their actions before drawing conclusions. Make a genuine effort to understand the detailed situation. This reveals the why behind the behavior.
- **Map the Situation.** Who are *all* the involved parties, and what are their motivations? Approach the situation like a high-stakes negotiation, and the results can be revealing.
- **Gather Complete Information.** Have you spoken with others who witnessed the behavior or incident? Ensure you have comprehensive information before making a judgment.
- **Align on Outcomes.** Identify the desired outcome and confirm that both you and your child understand it. Everyone makes mistakes, but limiting them to onetime occurrences prevents repetitive patterns.
- **Ensure Proportional Response.** If discipline is warranted, ensure the consequence matches the behavior. Overpunishing builds resentment. Maintain fairness, especially among siblings.

4

Raising Kids with Purpose

Purpose is not something we hand to our children; it's something we nurture, witness, and help them discover for themselves.

—HEATHER MALIN

Heather Malin, a Stanford researcher and author of *Teaching for Purpose*, has spent years studying how young people develop direction and meaning in their lives. Her research lands hard: Kids don't inherit purpose; they uncover it. But they only do so with the right support, environment, and room to explore—that's where we, as parents, come in.

A kid without purpose is like a Formula 1 car with no gas—powerful but going nowhere. Every child enters this world with raw potential humming just beneath the surface—untamed, unfiltered, waiting for ignition. Our job isn't to hand them a road map or force them into our lane. It's to give them enough open ground to run, fall, crash, and course-correct until they figure out what sets their soul on fire.

You may recall the puddle story from the introduction, in which I almost shouted at Tyler not to jump into that slushy, half-frozen mess that would inevitably lead to a sopping wet six-year-old covered in mud. But I didn't. That day, I caught myself almost crushing his instinct to explore, to play, to follow joy. The truth is, that's how purpose starts. It's not some magical calling or golden-light epiphany. It's a spark, buried in a mud puddle, a weird hobby, or some oddball question they ask that makes you stop and go, "Whoa, where did that come from?"

Malin and her team at Stanford did a multiyear longitudinal study following adolescents through their purpose development arc. They tracked 146 kids from middle school into college, and what they found should be a bullhorn wake-up call for every parent. At the start, most of the kids didn't have a polished vision of their future. They had feelings. Gut-level empathy. A desire to help, to contribute. One girl said she wanted to be the kind of person who "makes other people feel heard." Another wanted to be someone who "builds things that make life better." That's the purpose in the raw. Vague but real.

By high school, that sense of purpose started taking shape through exposure to new people, activities, struggles, and ideas. That's when these kids started saying things like "I want to become a teacher because I had one that changed my life," or "I want to be a doctor because I saw how much they helped when my grandfather got sick." They weren't just making noise. They were mapping meaning onto experiences.

By college, the kids who'd stuck with those sparks were actively building toward them: signing up for internships, picking majors with intention, and finding mentors. They weren't drifting. They were moving toward a purpose.

And here's the kicker: It wasn't the smartest or the most "disciplined" kids who stayed on course—it was the ones who had the most support and opportunities to explore, the ones who had been given a rich environment to reach their potential.

Malin's findings in *Teaching for Purpose* weren't shocking to anyone who's actually lived in the real world: Kids don't just "discover" purpose sitting in a classroom or listening to motivational talks. They find it through doing—by trying new things, hitting walls, building skills, and getting emotionally invested in something that feels bigger than themselves. Malin talks about this process as "pathway creation," and it's spot-on. Pathway creation is not about pushing them toward one ideal outcome; it's about giving them space and support to explore the terrain while helping them to keep going when it gets tough. We don't get to hand our kids their purpose wrapped in a bow. But we do get to shape the ground beneath their feet while they look for it.

A study by the Harvard Graduate School of Education found that nearly three in five young adults reported lacking meaning or purpose in their lives. This absence of direction can lead to feelings of anxiety and depression. As the Harvard Making Caring Common Report found, "Young adults in the U.S. report twice the rates of anxiety and depression as teens." That's an absolutely insane statistic to me, and it highlights the need for guidance and support in helping our children find their path.

Purpose isn't a luxury; it's a lifeline for our kids. It's the internal compass that helps them make sense of a complicated world, giving them direction when life gets messy (which it always does) and resilience when it gets hard. One of my favorite books on purpose is *Man's Search for Meaning*, by Viktor Frankl. Frankl wasn't just a psychiatrist; he was a Holocaust survivor who endured the unendurable. He spent years in Nazi concentration camps, stripped of his freedom, possessions, family, and nearly his life. In that crucible of suffering, he discovered something profound: Even when everything else is taken from us, the one thing that remains is our power to choose how we respond, to find meaning in the pain and suffering.

His insights weren't written from an ivory tower; they were carved out of starvation, loss, and brutality. That's what makes his message so powerful. Frankl teaches us that purpose isn't about comfort or achievement; it's about anchoring to something bigger than ourselves, something that can carry us even through the darkest storms. It's the reason I always look for brightness in the darkness, because if you look hard enough, the light is there.

Frankl wrote that those who have a why can endure almost any how; the same holds true for our children. Without purpose, they drift. With it, they endure, grow, and thrive. We must create the kind of environment where they can safely explore, stumble, and discover what lights them up. Because when a kid finds their purpose, they truly come alive. So how do we facilitate this journey? It starts with intentional conversations, exposure to travel, diverse experiences, and unwavering love and support.

Create an Environment Where They Can Find Their "Thing"

If there's one lesson I want you to remember throughout your parenting journey, it's that nobody is perfect, and you won't always have all the answers, but your default during challenging times should always be the same: Let your kids know you love them and are there for them. To do that, we must be present and engaged, which allows us to help our children uncover their passions and guide them toward a purposeful life. That kind of passion doesn't arrive in a clean, quiet package. It comes from skinned knees, burnt pancakes, broken bikes, and chasing after weird, wild ideas that don't always make sense to us parents on day one.

Have two or three crumb snatchers like I did, and you'll discover they're wired as differently as bourbon and kombucha. One might be a Lego warlord; the next could be jazz obsessed. When you spot that glint in their eye, lean in like you both found buried treasure and help them dig. I can't tell you how happy it made me when my kids would come to me with their crazy ideas or requests because I knew they were searching for their "thing," and that's wonderful to experience as a parent.

As discussed in chapter 2, environment is the name of the game. Just as you want to surround your kids with good people, you need to expose them to new experiences. Build an arena for them, not a playpen. Throw them into new sports, music class, art, science, chess, nature, travel, fashion, and more. And always look for good reasons for them to experience hard work and hardship along the way.

The environment to which you expose your kids also gives them a perspective they will carry through their lives as they discover themselves. One of the most powerful pieces of parenting advice I ever received came from a man who had every excuse not to be a parent, but he chose to do it anyway. A rabbi, who befriended me during my years living in New York, and his wife were unable to have children of their own due to medical complications. Instead, they opened their home and hearts to ten adopted kids. *Ten.* Every one of them came from a hard place, yet all but one grew into purposeful, passionate adults. The outlier? One son who fell into drug addiction, but even he eventually found his way back—a full recovery, a second chance. That experience alone proves how the environments we create, and the character-shaping moments within them, can anchor our kids for life.

Over coffee one fall afternoon in the Flatiron District, I asked the rabbi, Shalom, what his secret was. How had he raised so many kids, all of whom seemed to be thriving? He looked at me with eyes that had clearly seen joy and heartbreak in equal measure and said, "Brandon, if there's one thing you do as a father, one thing, take your children to a homeless shelter. Not on Thanksgiving. Not when the cameras are there or the feel-good volunteers show up in droves. Pick a regular, cold, miserable Tuesday in February. Show up with them. Serve food. Look people in the eye. Watch how it changes your kids. Watch how the warmth of helping someone in pain sticks with them more than any lecture or classroom lesson ever could."

He paused, then added, "That single act gave my children perspective. It grounded them. They saw, firsthand, how good they really had it, and how powerful it is to give."

I never forgot those words from Shalom. Still haven't. And I only wish I had taken advantage of that wisdom sooner. In a world obsessed with selfies and self-interest, perspective might just be the rarest, most valuable thing we can give our children. You can't force perspective or purpose on your kids; they must be unearthed. As parents, our job isn't to script their lives. Our job is to create a positive ecosystem where they can discover what lights them up, then support the hell out of it.

Make Sure It's Their Thing—Not Yours

I meet so many young people, and plenty of adults, adrift without any real sense of direction. They are smart and capable but untethered. Too often, there's a common thread running beneath the surface: Parents who pushed their own unfinished business onto their kids—dreams they never got to live, goals they never reached, passed down like unwanted weight. It's heartbreaking because that road leads to a harmful place—kids growing up feeling like no matter what they do, it's never really for *them*. It's for Mom. It's for Dad. Eventually, that pressure either breaks them or hardens them in the worst way, chasing a life that doesn't fit just to make someone else proud.

This is one of the biggest traps parents fall into, often without even realizing it—trying to relive their own unfulfilled dreams through their kids. The dad who never made it to the NBA suddenly has his son in year-round travel ball by age six. The mom who once chased a career in acting now has her daughter in vocal lessons and studio time every weekend.

Instead, we must guide our kids to help them find their *own* purpose. Pushing them to live out our lost dreams? That's not guidance. That's theft. It robs them of the chance to figure out who they are, on their own terms. I've seen it turn out badly more times than I care to count. For example, a friend of mine's spouse went to medical school, only to realize he became a doctor to make his parents happy. After a miserable residency, he gave up medicine to pursue an interest in private equity. His experience came at a great expense, and not just financial. Time is the one asset we can't earn back. If your kids' eyes don't light up like the Christmas tree at Rockefeller Center when you talk about specific interests, passions, or goals, then they're simply a distraction from the lives they could, and should, be living.

You're not their puppeteer; you're their guide. Help them discover their own fire; don't fan the embers of yours. Because nothing suffocates purpose faster than being handed a life that isn't yours to live. Don't get me wrong. There's nothing bad about sharing your passion with your kids—that's great, especially if they end up loving it. But unless your kid shows a genuine, self-driven love for that path, pushing your dream onto their shoulders is just a well-dressed form of control. And it almost always backfires. I saw this often while I coached Little League—I can't tell you how easy it was to spot the kid who didn't want to be on that baseball field.

Expose them to travel, different cultures, art, music, science, chess, computers, sports, languages. Let them build and break things in an effort to find their own thing. When the environment is right, passion becomes possible. And when they find that thing that makes them light up? That's the moment you step back and double down on your support.

Room to Explore

Sometimes when our kids want to experiment and have fun with life, we have to get out of our own damn way and let them live a little. That's mission critical. As parents, we don't create the fire; we stack the kindling and strike the match when we think the wind is just right. We have to let them try the sport, the language, the music, the coding class, the mud puddle! In our house, that meant exposure. Travel, camps, sports, art, drama, sailing, computers, whatever might strike a chord with them. Some things stuck, some didn't. But every new experience gave them a window into who they could become.

Jackson? He found his voice in the band room and sharpened it in speech and debate. His curiosity for tech turned him into a self-taught machine-learning engineer. That language immersion trip to Andalucía? Boom, fluent in Spanish, and it changed the way he saw the world.

Madison not only painted custom shoes in high school—which turned into that collaboration with Puma and Saks Fifth Avenue in New York and a legit business—she racked up scholarship offers from NYU and Parsons. She also shredded on the ski team and attended the Royal College of Art in London for her master's. Art wasn't just a hobby; it became her path.

And Tyler? The athlete and mathelete of the bunch. Basketball, golf, and math were his jam. Through years of exposure to my network—meeting other entrepreneurs, investors (like my close friend Kamal Ravikant), people building things—he got the bug for finance and showed an interest in investment banking. In September 2025, he started at the University of Oregon, where he is majoring in finance. Not bad for a kid who was on the verge of failing out of eighth grade.

As parents, we have to give our kids the room to explore. Let them develop their own why from the inside out. Because when they find it, it becomes the compass they carry for life. As mentioned, Malin and her team called this process "pathway creation." I call it raising kids who figure out what matters to them—and who chase it with everything they've got. So yeah, let them jump in the puddle, but don't forget to stand close enough to cheer when they find something deeper in the splash.

Encourage Them to Finish What They Start

When I was a young SEAL going through military free-fall parachute school in Yuma, Arizona, I watched a guy quit right before his first jump. We'd spent two weeks grinding through wind tunnel training at Fort Bragg, prepping for the real thing. The class was made up of Army Rangers, Green Berets, SEALs, and Marines. And on that first day in Yuma, we loaded into a twin-engine Osprey and flew 12,000 feet in the sky. The plan was simple: You jump solo, and an instructor dives out behind you to make sure you don't tumble to your death.

We got the signal from the jump master:

"Unbuckle!"

"Stand up!"

"Check equipment!"

The cabin filled with a roar as the ramp began to lower with the warm desert air flooding in. You could smell the dry scent of sand and sage, even from thousands of feet above the Yuma desert. The horizon stretched forever, the sun blazing over a sea of mud-colored earth and jagged desert mountains.

I watched as the Army guy next to me pushed himself up, shuffled closer to the edge, and glanced down at the endless open sky and desert floor far below. For a split second, time froze . . . then he sat back down hard, clipped his belt back in, and shook his head back and forth. It was a hard pass.

That was it. He was done. After I ran off the ramp, with the rest of my life depending on pulling that chute, I never saw him again. To this day, I wonder what kind of childhood, what kind of foundation, or lack of it, made quitting in a moment like that feel like the only option. That choice likely cost him his military career. But even worse, it probably carved a scar into how he saw himself every time he thought about that day.

Purpose isn't a one-and-done deal. It changes. It *should* change. As your kids reach their goals, grow older, and step into new stages of life, the thing that lights them up in their early twenties may not be the same thing that fuels them at thirty. And that's OK. In fact, it's normal. I tell my kids it's just as important to look ahead to their next purpose or goal as it is to chase the one in front of them. I've watched too many friends sell a business or reach a huge milestone, only to spiral afterward because they never planned for what came next. Purpose isn't a trophy you put on a shelf; it's a torch you keep carrying into the next chapter of your life.

But of course, with new goals, passions, and purposes come new skills. And learning something new can be tough. This is where I see some parents flinch. I call it "the dip," that ugly middle zone where the new endeavor gets hard and uncomfortable, and your kid wants to quit. It's easy to confuse passion with ease, especially when we're young, but anything worth doing is usually difficult before it clicks. As you expose your kids to the world, you still need to hold the line when they experience resistance and want the easy out. That might mean you have to push them through the suck of learning something new, especially when they begged to start it in the first place.

I remember when I first taught my kids to ski. I enrolled them in half-day ski and snowboard classes. Then after their class was over for the day, I'd take them on the gondola to the top of the mountain for some dad lessons. Day one was excitement. Day two was tears, sore legs, and nonstop complaining about the cold. By day four, they were bargaining to skip the mountain and "just do hot chocolate and play video games at home or swim at the rec center."

Sometimes I just wanted to say screw it and pack it up. But I knew what was coming—that beautiful turning point where they would get over the hump of learning something new, when skill meets confidence and everything falls into place. At the end of the week, they were flying down the slopes like they'd been born in the Swiss Alps.

This only happened because I didn't let them bail when things got tough. Sometimes, the most loving thing we can do is gently close the exit door when our kids want to walk through it too soon. This isn't punishment; there is value in finishing what we start. As adults, we have the experience to know what's waiting on the other side of discomfort: skill, confidence, and growth. So when my kids hit that inevitable wall halfway through their ski lessons and wanted to call it, I didn't let them walk away. Not because I was being hard on them, but because I've seen firsthand what quitting can steal from a person, like that soldier who couldn't bring himself to leap from that plane into the unknown.

I don't care about perfect attendance or checking boxes; what I care about is never letting my kids carry the weight of wondering what might've happened if they had just stood up and jumped. That's the real lesson. That's the gift hidden inside discipline: knowing you didn't retreat when it got uncomfortable. You leaned in. You finished. And you came out stronger.

Once you teach them the importance of finishing what they start, then they can stop if it's not what they want. Help them recognize that sometimes, we have to get to the other side of the finish line to really understand if this is for us or not.

The other night, I was sitting at dinner with Jackson at one of our favorite restaurants, Brihlante, in Lisbon, where I now live. Out of the blue, he looked up from his plate and said, "Dad, thanks for pushing me with the ski lessons back then." It stopped me in my tracks. That moment, simple as it was, reminded me why we do the hard stuff as parents—that's the payoff. That's the beautiful return on all those times I didn't let them give up. Sometimes, the most important thing you can teach your kid is not how to be great at something; it's how to finish something.

Now, years later, skiing isn't just a skill; it's one of the things that brings us together, a shared activity we can do that has lasted far beyond when the kids left the house. Our ski trips have become a tradition we all look forward to. There's something special about being on the mountain together, the fresh cold air, the beauty of the outdoors, cheering each other on down the slopes. It's where we reconnect and can just be a family.

The belief that you can push through discomfort and come out stronger on the other side is a muscle, and it only grows when you exercise it at the music lesson or game, when you finish the season, when you do the work. You're not being mean; you're building their backbone. Passion needs pressure. Teaching them how to set goals and achieve them from an early age is such a gift. As shown in chapter 2, confidence needs repetition. And purpose? Purpose is what's waiting at the top of that ski hill, once they've earned the view.

Teach Them to Plan Their Life, and Live Their Plan

I've always been a dreamer. But when I joined the military, the dreamer in me became a doer as well. The Navy instilled structure and taught me how to execute on a sharp to-do list and create a strategy around the future. Even before then, though, my father taught me a valuable lesson about execution. I was fifteen. I still remember sitting around the small dinner table aboard our ketch *Agio*. My dad put down his fork, looked at the family, and announced that he didn't want to be another sailor in the harbor, always talking about the trip never taken. You could hear the weight in his voice, the quiet frustration of dreams deferred, and the conviction that followed.

That was his moment of truth, the push that turned "someday" into a plan. Not long after, our family set sail from Ventura, California, bound for New Zealand. It wasn't perfect timing, it wasn't perfect preparation, but it was enough. Once we left the harbor, the adventure became real. (If only I knew what was coming!)

My dad's lesson stuck with me. Dreams don't happen when you wait for perfect; they happen when you're willing to untie the lines and just fucking go. This is something I also wanted to teach my kids, because I've benefited so much from making strategic thinking and goal-setting a lifetime habit. How to set goals—not just wishful thinking or vague ideas but real goals with direction and intention behind them—is a powerful habit to develop at an early age.

Planning your life, or not, is the difference between floating down the river with a paddle in hand or just drifting along, going where outside forces push you. I prefer holding that paddle with a planned destination in mind. The journey may be challenging, but at least I know where I'm headed.

Plan your life, live your plan.

Teaching your kids how to set goals and follow through is a lesson that will stick with them throughout their lives, allowing them to not just realize but actualize their purpose. To that end, every year over Christmas school break—while most families are busy tripping over wrapping paper and trying to keep the peace with the relatives (we all have at least one of those family members!)—I started a new family tradition. I sat down with each of my kids and helped them write up a mini mission brief for the year ahead, focusing on school, personal, family, and three-year goals.

If they were stuck, I'd ask questions to get them thinking. "What do you want to accomplish this year? What challenge scares you but still excites you?" I tried to keep it simple, raw, and honest, but I also made sure the goals were measurable, specific, and actionable. For example, as opposed to "I want to lose weight this year," a goal that is measurable, specific, and actionable might be "I want to lose five pounds by the end of May."

Sometimes their goals were accomplishment based, like "winning a round of speech and debate this year" or "learning how to play a new song on the guitar before summer starts." For goals like "I want the new iPhone," we'd talk about what they needed to do to make that happen. I actually loved when they brought up the latter type of goals—a new phone, a special pair of headphones—because I knew it was a chance to introduce some "dad leverage," which would usually come with a reading or learning assignment.

I'd make them write their mission out on their phones, and we'd always check their goals from the previous year when planning for the next one. If they achieved one over the prior twelve months as planned, we celebrated like they just won a gold medal.

That tradition created ownership, conditioning my kids to think about the future and how they wanted to shape it. It gave them a reason to push, to track progress, and to feel that primal satisfaction that only comes from earning something—no handouts, participation trophies, or "good job" stickers, just a moment where they could look in the mirror and say, "Whoa—I did that!"

I was digging through my old iNotes the other day, chasing down something completely unrelated, when I stumbled on a little time capsule. Titled "Webb Family Goal Planning, 2018," there they were: Madison's, Tyler's, and Jackson's personal goals and vision statements, written in their own words at a time when they were still figuring out who they were and what they cared about. Reading through them now, years later, with the benefit of hindsight—and pride—it's incredible to see how much of who they are was already taking shape back then. These weren't just bullet points; they were breadcrumbs on the trail to becoming the people they are now.

Let's start with Madison's.

Madison

Vision Statement

I will continue to strive to be the best I can possibly be. To do so, I will achieve my goals and create new and greater goals. I will listen to others' advice and use it to grow into a better person while leading by example. I will strive to influence the people around me. I will continue to learn new things and use my knowledge to help others. I will be considerate to others and help make the world a better place.

Goals

School

1. Continue to learn Spanish and succeed
2. Continue to get good grades (93% or higher)
3. Be excited by learning (create an independent study or project)

Personal

1. Join the Lincoln ski team in high school
2. Help out with the girls [her younger sisters Gretchen had with her new husband] at least once a week
3. Sign up for the ski bus

Family

1. FaceTime or call Dad at least four times a week
2. Be supportive and encouraging to siblings (e.g., go to Tyler's soccer and basketball games, do debate with Jackson)
3. Continue the skiing tradition with family

Three-Year Goals

1. Have my license
2. Make money by babysitting
3. Maintain a 4.0 GPA
4. Make new friends
5. Stay close with family
6. Be on Lincoln ski team
7. Continue skiing tradition with family

Tyler

Vision Statement

My name is Tyler. I will be a leader and have people look up to me for who I am and what I can do on the court. I will be happy and have a great family that wakes up every day in a nice bed. I will be a successful man and have a good business that helps people around me. I will leave this earth with a dent.

Goals

School

1. Get good grades on my report card (90% or higher)
2. Make five new friends by January 17
3. Take the ski bus with one friend in middle school

Personal

1. Be a great basketball player
2. Work harder at everything
3. Make a higher team in basketball

Family

1. Be a better leader to my [younger] sisters
2. Help out more around the house
3. Don't bicker as much

Three-Year Goals

1. Have a good grade in math
2. Be friends with a lot of people
3. Be faster, stronger, and healthier

Jackson

Vision Statement

I want to be the type of person who:

1. Is valued for their hard work in groups and as an individual
2. Is an avid learner who spends time in impactful ways
3. Accepts responsibility and fulfills expectations
4. Accepts failure in myself and others and moves forward to succeed

5. People enjoy being around
6. Is respectful and open to new ideas without criticism
7. DOESN'T PROCRASTINATE and is HEALTHY in all aspects, especially without stress

Goals

School

1. Maintain a 4.0 GPA, but most of all, strive to learn
2. Win in a speech and debate tournament
3. Attend Stanford summer debate camp
4. Challenge myself with honors classes

Personal

1. Start and maintain a bullet journal to stay organized
2. Dedicate myself and embrace the culture in Spain; learn a lot of Spanish and have a great experience
3. Learn to play piano, especially "Rhapsody in Blue"
4. Read a little every night
5. Surround myself with content that's both entertaining and educational
6. Spend more time volunteering, doing things I enjoy
7. Read the news every day at breakfast

Family

1. When I make promises, I fulfill them
2. Choose to go out with family rather than stay home
3. Be a good role model to my siblings

Three-Year Goals

1. Be in a college where I'll enjoy myself and pursue my passion
2. Have a driver's license
3. Pursue passion projects that I plan
4. Land an internship

5. Have some form of income
6. Be in a healthy relationship

The Follow-Through

You'll notice how grounded and achievable their goals were—nothing flashy or impossible, just real, tangible stepping stones that reflected who they were and what they cared about at the time. If you decide to make goal-setting a family tradition, take the same approach: Keep it simple, keep it personal, and let the goals come from them. You shouldn't be scripting their life for them here; you should be helping them learn how to write it. (And to help you in the process, I've provided a goal-setting template in the Parenting Resources section at the end of the book.)

There's real magic when your kid starts seeing themselves follow through—their confidence skyrockets. They realize they're not just dreaming; they're building. Looking at where my kids are today, it's incredible to see how those early seeds have grown. So let me show you where they've landed, each on their own path, fueled by purpose, discipline, and the freedom to chase what mattered most to them:

- **Madison** achieved just about every goal she set for herself. She graduated from Lincoln High School with a 4.3 GPA and completed her undergrad with honors at Goldsmiths. She became fluent in Spanish, made the Lincoln ski team, and was a regular on the ski bus, just like she envisioned. Still the steady, supportive big sister, she continued to help out with her younger siblings while pursuing her master's degree at the prestigious Royal College of Art in London.
- **Tyler** hit his stride on and off the court. He made the travel basketball team in Portland, held a 3.0 grade average throughout high school, and has grown into a thoughtful and dependable older brother for his two younger sisters. In the summer of

2026, he'll finish his freshman year at the University of Oregon, bringing that quiet determination and leadership he's carried from the start.

- **Jackson** has stayed true to his passion for learning and self-improvement. He scored that internship he set his sights on and graduated with honors from the University of St. Andrews. He is now the founder of a fast-growing property tech start-up called LandLord (uselandlord.com), which uses artificial intelligence to help owners manage properties worldwide. While his siblings love to tease him that he still hasn't gotten his driver's license, he continues to chase bigger goals with purpose, vision, and drive.

After rereading my kids' old goal lists and seeing how much they'd actually accomplished, I did some digging. What I found was this: We weren't just building family rituals with this yearly goal-setting tradition—we were following a high-performance strategy, whether we knew it or not. Dr. Gail Matthews, a psychologist at Dominican University of California, conducted a landmark study that showed people who write down their goals are over 40 percent more likely to achieve them than those who don't. Let that sink in for a second. The simple act of writing it down gives you a *40 percent* edge. That's not positive thinking—that's a tactical advantage.

But it doesn't stop there. When those goals are shared with someone who helps keep you accountable, your chances of success skyrocket even further. That's not luck—that's intention turned into momentum, resulting in execution. When I sat down with my kids every year to write down goals together, I was laying the groundwork for teaching them how to dream with discipline, act on what matters, and build a habit of achievement, not just on paper, but in real life.

What a gift it was to stumble across those old iNotes when doing research for this book. Reading through those digital time capsules holding each of my kids' goals from all those years ago felt like opening a letter from the past, not just from my children, but from the adults they were becoming. The part that affected me hardest? Most of the goals they wrote down—some bold, some humble, some playful—they actually achieved. It wasn't about perfection. It was about direction. And that, to me, is the real power of goal-setting.

The Follow-Up

After writing this chapter, I went back to my kids and asked them some honest questions about how they experienced my parenting. I wasn't fishing for praise or looking to relive the highlight reel; I wanted the truth. The real impact. The good, the bad, the "I wish you'd done it differently."

Here are the three questions I asked each of them:

1. What's one thing I did as a parent that really stuck with you, for better or worse?
2. Was there ever a time you wished I'd handled something differently? What would that have looked like to you?
3. If you had to describe my parenting style in one sentence to your friends, what would you say?

They wrote down their answers, and here's how they replied:

Jackson's Answers

What stuck: "Letting me take the subway by myself to my internship in NYC. I knew Mom would never let me do it, and it made me feel like I needed to step up to meet the responsibility you trusted in me. Instead of rebelling against parenting, I got to rise to it."

What he wished I'd done differently: "I wish one of you had sat me down and taught me how to file taxes. Even if I didn't make much money at the time, it would've been helpful just to understand it early. It's not hard once you know how, but I had to figure it out the long way."

Parenting style in a sentence: "Cool-headed, disciplined, adventurous."

Tyler's Answers

What stuck: "Traveling and seeing new places really shaped me. It taught me how to adjust when I felt uncomfortable or out of place. I used that when I had to switch schools. I didn't shut down, I adapted and figured it out."

What he wished I'd done differently: "When we were younger, I think work pulled you away a lot. Back then, I didn't really get it, but looking back, I do wish you'd been around a little more. That said, I've noticed how much better you've gotten at being present now, and I really appreciate that."

Parenting style in a sentence: "You let me figure things out on my own but stepped in when I needed it."

Madison's Answers

What stuck: "I was eighteen, trying to act like an adult, doing the dishes, and I broke one of your glasses. I looked at you, expecting you to be mad. You looked up from your chess game, took a sip of your drink, and said, 'It's just a glass. I'll get a new one.' That moment showed me how to pause and think before reacting. A lot of people go straight to emotion or blame. You taught us that the small stuff is small, and the big stuff deserves our real attention."

What she wished I'd done differently: "You were our ski-champion, surfing, skydiving hero. We admire you more than you'll ever know. But I think hearing more about your failures, your mistakes, your embarrassing moments would've made us more comfortable with our own. We didn't need you to be perfect. We needed to know you weren't always perfect either."

Parenting style in a sentence: "Real. Honest. Give life your best, because that's what it'll give back. It's OK to make mistakes, but don't look like a garage sale while you're at it."

These three conversations reminded me that our kids are always watching. Always remembering. When we're lucky enough to hear the impact from their side of the story, we get a glimpse of what actually mattered to them and should have mattered to us. Reading their words was emotional. There's a brutal honesty in your kids' reflections that no parenting book can prepare you for. But what I found between the lines, through the regrets, the compliments, the little gaps I didn't even realize were there, was this: The foundation we built together was strong. Not flawless. But real. And real holds up.

Field Note: Let Them Write Their Own Story

- Don't hand them your map; help them draw their own.
- Follow the spark. Give them the time and tools necessary to explore what genuinely interests them.
- Varied, real-life experience beats megaphones. One positive experience can change a trajectory.

Family Challenge: Ask, "What's one thing you're curious about right now?" Schedule a one-hour deep-dive talk with your kid this week.

Advice from Madison: *My advice? Don't sweat the small stuff. When parents stay calm over life's little accidents, it teaches us to do the same and saves the energy for the stuff that actually matters.*

Chapter Checklist

- **Create Space for Exploration.** Expose your kids to new experiences, sports, art, travel, science, music, and hard work, so they can discover what lights them up.
- **Encourage Them to Finish What They Start.** Teach them that pushing through the "dip" builds resilience, confidence, and grit.
- **Separate Your Dreams from Theirs.** Support their passions but don't hand them your unfinished business.
- **Make Goal-Setting a Family Ritual.** Write goals down together each year—research shows it increases achievement by over 40 percent.
- **Normalize Failure.** Share your own stumbles and comebacks so they see failure as a step, not a dead end.
- **Provide Perspective.** Expose them to service, hardship, and diverse communities so they develop empathy and gratitude.
- **Keep Purpose Flexible.** Remind them that what drives them at fifteen may change at twenty-five, and that's healthy.

5

Modeling Healthy Habits

Let food be thy medicine and medicine be thy food.

—HIPPOCRATES

Hippocrates, often called the "Father of Modern Medicine," was a Greek physician, born around 460 BCE, whose teachings laid the foundation for medical ethics and clinical practice. He believed in treating the whole person—mind, body, and environment—not just a person's symptoms. His ancient advice—let food be thy medicine and medicine be thy food—still holds up. How we forgot this lesson in modern Western society is a mystery to me, but it seems like we're finally catching on to Hippocrates' wisdom again, even if it's 2,400 years later. This gives me hope for humanity.

You can see the shift everywhere: schools swapping out vending machines for healthier snacks, professional athletes preaching clean eating and recovery, entire grocery aisles dedicated to plant-based or organic foods, and doctors prescribing lifestyle changes before pills. The fact that "farm-to-table" and "whole foods" are no longer fringe terms tells me we're recalling what Hippocrates knew all along: The fuel you put in your body sets the stage for long-term health.

In the SEAL Teams, you train to extremes in BUD/S and on active duty. You learn to survive on fumes, to function in the red and beyond, all to discover how far you can truly push your mind and body. What I discovered is that most people operate at a one or two out of ten, and they don't even know it. In BUD/S training, the days would blur together with barely any sleep—our bodies wrecked, our minds unraveling by the minute—and still, we were expected to carry on through twelve-foot surf and rip currents like it was just another Tuesday.

And we did.

The training stripped us down to our rawest selves, forcing us to confront the question, What's left? How far can you go when your tank's empty and the mission still matters? Will you give up or drive on until you collapse? The SEALs want people who will never quit, no matter the odds. This drive is proven, or broken, in the modern crucible of SEAL training. Over 220 started in my class—only 23 of us originals made it to the end.

Then there's Hell Week, where instructors keep you up for over five days straight, training under hazardous conditions throughout. These guys were part sadist, part showman, part mad scientist. One minute they're hosing you down in freezing surf at 3 a.m., the next they're marching you through the soft sand like some deranged desert caravan. Sleep is dangled in front of you like a carrot, then yanked away the second you start to close your eyes. It's chaos carefully designed to snap you in two, physically and mentally.

A few days before Hell Week kicked off, I was already beaten down, exhausted, and walking on a razor's edge. One afternoon during First Phase, we'd been hauling heavy rubber boats on our heads from the storage area in the training compound to the beach and back again and again. Suddenly, instructor Shoulin pointed at me. My crew froze. Shoulin barked, "Webb, get over here." I knew that tone; I was screwed.

He and three other instructors marched me away, the four of them circling me like sharks with blood in the water. Then they dropped a harsh punishment on me for being one of the weak physical links in the class: a hundred eight-count bodybuilders—consisting of push-up stance, scissor kicks, and squat thrusts—all while they shoved sand in my face and screamed the whole time. "You are a worthless piece of shit!" they roared. "No one wants you here!" For an hour, I kept going, legs trembling, lungs burning, while my classmates wondered what happened to me. It was a severe beating designed to get me to quit—only I didn't.

They tore me apart to see if I'd break. But what I realized during that hellish hour is that every move was still a choice. Near the end of the torture, I yelled out, "I am not leaving here unless it's in a body bag, I have nowhere else to GO!" like in the movie *An Officer and a Gentleman*. By the time they sent me back to my boat crew, I wasn't just physically ready; I was mentally locked in. And from that moment on, they never messed with me again.

When Hell Week started a few days later, I was still in pain, but everything seemed easy. My mindset had shifted—I was no longer the guy running from failure; I'd already stood at the edge and chosen to continue.

What does this have to do with ancient Greek philosophers and food?

There was no way my fellow SEALs hopefuls and I could train that hard without fueling the machine. During BUD/S, especially Hell Week, we were burning upwards of 6,000 to 7,000 calories per day. Some guys even shed 8,000 depending on their metabolism. The human body simply can't take that kind of punishment without *real* fuel. We ate like starving dogs: massive trays of eggs, potatoes, pasta, peanut butter, anything put in front of us. It wasn't about diet trends or macros; it was about survival. That level of output demands serious input. If you didn't eat, you broke down. If you didn't hydrate, you passed out. And you can't pour junk in the tank and expect a high-performance engine to run.

The same goes for our kids. This struck me with clarity one blurry-eyed morning in La Jolla. Jackson had barely slept the night before. For breakfast, he shoveled a bowl of sugar-soaked cereal down his throat and then melted down like the Chernobyl reactor before we even backed out of the driveway. I felt the frustration bubbling up, but then I had a flashback to the Teams. The Navy wouldn't send a SEAL Team into a high-stakes op without proper food and rest, so why the hell was I sending a seven-year-old into his daily mission at elementary school with less than that?

Nutrition and sleep aren't luxuries. They're the unsexy, non-negotiable foundation of resilience, focus, emotional regulation, and even self-worth. It all starts with a well-rested brain and a body that's actually been fed, not just filled. When our kids get that right, they don't just "behave" better, they thrive. They move through the world sharper, calmer, and more confident. They smile more. They suffer less. But unless we model these healthy habits for our children, they're unlikely to ever adopt them on their own.

The Challenges to Healthy Living

The challenges we deal with as parents trying to get our kids to eat healthy and get adequate rest start with their peers and well-meaning but misinformed (or lazy) adults. Then there are the terrible, unhealthy school lunches and vending machines that dish out sugar. As if these obstacles weren't enough, we also have to contend with the crap being peddled to our kids by Madison Avenue's finest marketing agencies through TikTok and other online platforms.

A recent study from the Center for Science in the Public Interest found that 63 percent of teens use TikTok, and nearly 70 percent of branded food videos they watch don't disclose they're paid ads. That means our kids see junk-food ads and think they're genuine recommendations. They are being fed garbage, literally and psychologically, without even realizing it. Junk food in, junk mindset out. Advertising agencies for "Big Food" brands also commonly toss words like "whole grain," "antioxidant," "gluten-free," or "low-fat" onto packages to generate a false sense of health for both kids and adults. But remember, cocaine and meth are also gluten-free and vegan—buyer beware.

Still, I've come to realize that the first institution to mislead me about what constitutes actual healthy food wasn't some major corporation, but the US government. Remember the food pyramid most of us '80s kids were spoon-fed in school? Absolute trash. A government-sponsored hallucination built on sugar, artificially flavored cereal, and Big Food lobbyist dollars. We were told to fill up on white bread like we were carb-loading for the Boston Marathon and treat fat like it was radioactive waste. Meanwhile, Kellogg's and Nabisco were laughing all the way to the bank. It wasn't nutrition—it was nutritional theater, a pyramid-shaped lie that left a whole generation wired, inflamed, and wondering why they couldn't focus by third period.

America is a great country, but let's be honest, we can be our own worst enemy. That's especially true when it comes to what we allow into our food supply. We wave the flag for freedom, yet most Americans have no idea that some of the foods they eat daily wouldn't even be allowed on grocery store shelves across Europe. Over 160 food and drug ingredients approved by the FDA in the US are banned or heavily restricted in the European Union due to health concerns. We're talking about common additives like brominated vegetable oil (BVO), used in sports drinks and sodas (banned in Europe and Japan but still lurking in US products). Or take potassium bromate, a dough conditioner used in white breads and pizza crusts that's been linked to cancer in lab animals—that one's outlawed in the UK, Canada, and the EU, but not in the good ole US of A.

Even Red 40 and Yellow 5—artificial food dyes found in cereal, candy, salad dressings, and many foods in between—are flagged overseas and require warning labels in Europe because of their link to hyperactivity in children. Here? They're handed out like candy on Halloween (which is, of course, full of these dyes). Our kids are being fed stuff that wouldn't clear customs in half the developed world, and it's not because we lack the science to back up the facts. It's because we've let profits and lobbyists steer the ship while health takes a backseat.

But change may finally be stirring. The FDA and HHS recently announced plans to phase out petroleum-based synthetic dyes from the food supply, signaling that the law may soon catch up with what science has long known. If that shift becomes reality, this book, and the choices you make in your kitchen, will already be on the right side of history.

It's time we paid attention to what we're feeding the next generation. This isn't about fearmongering—it's about waking up. If you want to raise strong, resilient kids, you need to start with what's on their plate. If you can't read all the ingredients on the package or don't know what half of them are, you shouldn't be feeding that product to your kids (and you shouldn't be eating it either). You wouldn't pump cheap gas into a Porsche. Why fuel your child—your most valuable asset—with garbage?

If you ever want to see a horrifying time-lapse of American health decline, go online and look for this meme (there's more than one version): a side-by-side photo comparison of Americans at the beach in the 1980s next to one from today. The '80s crew looks like a beer-commercial softball team—tanned, lean, shirtless guys with big hair and no body fat. With today's photo, you'd swear someone hijacked a Carnival Cruise food buffet. It's a wall of flesh: tank tops, belly rolls, sunburned sausage fingers clutching 64-ounce sodas.

I grew up in a leaner era. In the '80s, we rode bikes without helmets, ate food that actually came from the ground or the butcher, and treated soda as an occasional treat, not a daily IV drip of liquid sugar. Back then, type 2 diabetes and cancer felt like rare tragedies you might hear about in hushed tones, not everyday conditions woven into the background of modern life. Fast-forward and the numbers tell the story: According to the CDC, the prevalence of diagnosed diabetes in US adults jumped from about 9.7 percent in 1999–2000 to 14.3 percent in 2021–2023. Cancer is no outlier either: Over 1.85 million new cases were reported in 2022 alone. What was once rare is now common.

Influencing our kids' eating habits is one of the most challenging things we as parents will face. As we battle our own bad habits, our children are watching. We are up against social media, cheap fast food, and New York's brightest food marketers that could sell holy water to the Vatican. If you're not already living in a healthy food household, you're going to have to learn what it is to eat healthy and model these practices for your children. In the end, you'll thank me for it.

Healthy Eating Starts at Home

As a newbie teacher at the sniper program, I'd occasionally be given a topic to teach that I wasn't exactly an expert on, so I had to become one quickly. Take ballistics. Sure, I knew the basics, but I couldn't have told you that a .300 Win Mag sniper rifle has a 1:10 twist rate for a 190-grain bullet. Teaching a new subject takes a lot of study and preparation in order to present the material with confidence to a class. As parents, sometimes our job is to become experts in a new subject in order to teach our children. And don't think you can fake it to your kids these days—they'll use ChatGPT on you!

When it comes to nutrition and food, I always thought I knew what it was like to eat healthy, but as a young parent, I found out I didn't know crapola. My moment of clarity—as recovering addicts call it—happened when I was a twentysomething SEAL at SEAL Team 3 in Coronado, California. It was an unusually warm summer in 2000, and I was at a house party in Encinitas with my friend Glen "Bub" Doherty (KIA, Benghazi, Libya). I happened to overhear a woman named Lisa talking about how she had beaten breast cancer by changing her diet.

I was curious. I leaned into Lisa's conversation with a cold IPA in hand and stepped a little closer so I could hear better. Turns out she'd read a book called *The China Study*, a nutrition manifesto built on decades of research (not some TikTok fad). In the 2005 book,

Cornell PhD biochemist T. Colin Campbell and his son dive into the China–Cornell–Oxford Project: an epidemiological sweep across sixty-five rural Chinese counties in the early 1980s. These researchers surveyed 6,500 adults—recording bloodwork, death rates, and dietary logs—and mapped every correlation between what people ate and the diseases that killed them.

Campbell's bombshell claim: Diets heavy in animal protein—including meat, milk, cheese, and eggs—were tied to higher rates of cancer, heart disease, diabetes, and other diseases. Conversely, the more whole, unprocessed plant-based foods people ate, the healthier they were, period. There was no threshold where the benefits stopped. The healthiest communities ate up to 90 percent plant-based diets, with 10 percent or less animal-based proteins, and saw dramatically fewer of these "rich country diseases."

Campbell didn't just highlight these findings and walk away. He weathered an onslaught from "Big Food" lobbyists—the meat, dairy, and processed food industries that had skin in the game. They funded critics, cherry-picked data to discredit his conclusions, and downplayed his study using PR tactics straight out of the tobacco playbook, sowing confusion and doubt. But Campbell stuck to the facts: no flashy diet, no celebrity gimmick, just science-backed discipline at the dinner table.

Campbell has argued that nutrition is routinely sidelined in medical training, which is part of why he took his decades of research to a broader audience. When *The China Study* came out, it challenged a lot of nutritional orthodoxy. Some critics dismissed Campbell's conclusions as overreach, while others embraced the work and its implications.

Lisa took Campbell's advice to heart, and guess what? She healed herself with diet alone. Not because she took some magic pill or chemo but because she stopped feeding the disease and started fueling her body the way God intended. After hearing Lisa talk about her experience, I read the book, and it crushed me like a knock-out punch from Floyd "The Money" Mayweather.

It wasn't Campbell's story that got me; it was the data and science behind it. He also wasn't selling his readers anything. His passion for the subject—to share the science and expose the bullshit around the American diet—shone through on every page. His work made it clear that we'd let food capitalism run us off the healthy eating cliff. Big lobbyists have pushed their agenda through our government, and Madison Avenue's advertising agencies have redefined what it means to eat healthy. Meanwhile, there has been no real incentive to fix this growing problem.

Whether we'd like to admit it or not, the US government and good old-fashioned capitalism can sometimes lead us astray. If you have your doubts, just take a moment to look up some of the marketing from the 1950s advocating for healthy cigarettes. These are three 1950s cigarette advertising quotes I pulled from a quick online search:

- **"More doctors smoke Camels than any other cigarette."—Camel ad, 1946–1950s.** This was part of a nationwide ad campaign that featured physicians in lab coats recommending cigarettes.
- **"Give your throat a vacation . . . Smoke a fresh cigarette."—Lucky Strike ad, 1950s.** Yes, they were literally promoting cigarettes as a way to soothe your throat.
- **"Scientific evidence on effects of smoking: no adverse effects on nose, throat, or sinuses."—Philip Morris ad, late 1940s.** Backed by "science"—bought and paid for, of course.

The ugly truth few people want to admit is that the American food supply has been hijacked. We are all eating GMO frankenfood. Corn syrup in every package. Processed garbage so loaded with chemicals it might as well come with a Surgeon General's warning and a Groupon for insulin. And we're feeding it to our kids—especially in school lunches—like it's safe and normal.

It's not.

Want to raise healthy kids? Start with what you and they eat. A healthy lifestyle doesn't come from the junk food marketed to our children. It comes from real, whole food—truly organic whenever possible—and a mostly plant-based diet. These fuel energy, clarity, and control, which can't be faked when your bloodstream's choked with sugar and preservatives. Just look at the Blue Zones, those rare places in the world where people regularly live past a hundred. What do they have in common? One major aspect is a diet built on vegetables, legumes, whole grains, and little processed junk. They've proven what Hippocrates said 2,400 years ago: Food is medicine. And if it works for them, it can work for us and our kids too.

Food is probably one of the toughest aspects of parenting to tackle because there are so many external food factors outside of our control once our kids are with friends or at school. But it starts at home; we have to model good eating habits ourselves. Kids learn from what they see and hear. They eat what you eat and what's available to them. If you hammer down a bag of Doritos every night as a coping strategy, don't be surprised when your kid follows suit and ends up having to take insulin for life.

We are what we eat, and our job as parents is to figure out a clever way to drive that point home to our kids. Most things in life don't mean crap to us or our kids unless there is relevance and value attached to them. And sometimes we have to be sneaky in how we nudge our kids in the direction we know is best for them—the message might even hit better when it doesn't come from Mom or Dad. It can be a camp, a better peer group, a coach delivering the message, a book, or a sports hero advocating for eating healthy. Think of ways to surround your kids with positive, healthy eating behaviors and role models.

Still, try your best not to become a food "dictator," ordering your kids into healthier food habits. If you do, your kids will just find a way to eat around your strict rules. I always let mine have a few treats, kind of like letting a balloon squeak out some air before it pops. A little sugar here and there kept the peace—and kept me from being overthrown in a snack-related coup.

"Sleep Is a Goddamn Weapon"

In the SEAL Teams, our body was our first weapon. If you treated it like a junkyard, it didn't matter how fit you were; you were a liability. Like any Olympic athlete understands, without eating an optimal diet, you won't perform at an optimal level. As parents, when it comes to our family's health, what we feed ourselves and our children is extremely important—but so is a good night's sleep.

As my first platoon chief, Dan, used to growl at us new guys: "Sleep is a goddamn weapon, boys." At the time, I thought he was just being dramatic, but I came to understand that sleep deprivation turns even the hardest of men into emotional toddlers with motor skills of a drunk Russian.

Now apply that reality to your kid.

Sleep isn't a luxury; it's crucial maintenance. While your child's body is down for the count, the real work begins: Growth hormones get released, brain wiring strengthens, the immune system becomes fortified, and the complexity of the day gets sorted into long-term memory. A major study out of the University of Maryland School of Medicine found that kids who don't get enough sleep show elevated risk of behavioral issues that mirror ADHD—we're talking impulsivity, short fuses, lack of focus, and a brain firing like a laptop with thirty-seven tabs open. Add chronic sleep deprivation and you've got a recipe for stunted growth, weakened immune function, and the emotional regulation of a caffeinated ferret.

But give a kid consistent, high-quality sleep? Improved concentration, better problem-solving, smoother emotional control, and, you guessed it, stronger relationships and school performance. Well-rested kids are literally more coachable, more resilient, and more themselves. So set the bedtime routine and kill the screens because sleep *is* a weapon, as much as healthy eating.

Case Study: The Clear Effect of an Organic Diet on Kids

A 2024 peer-reviewed study out of *Environmental Health Perspectives* tracked the diets of forty American kids between the ages of three and six, half from urban Oakland, the other half from the farming belt in Salinas Valley. In the study, the researchers made one simple change: They swapped the kids' usual, nonorganic diets for organic food and then measured what kind of chemical crap was floating around in their systems before and after.

The results? Brutal—in a good way. Ever heard of organophosphate pesticides? These brain-toxic chemicals were originally designed for insect control but have found their way into our food and can mess with the human nervous system—kids are especially vulnerable. Within just a few days of the swap, levels of two organophosphate pesticides fell by 40 percent and 49 percent. That's not subtle; that's a biological mic drop. Even the herbicide 2,4-D—yep, the same weedkiller linked to cancer—plummeted by 25 percent. No special detox, no magic powders, no Alex Jones tinfoil conspiracy talk—cleaner food led to less poison in their system.

When our kids follow the typical American diet, they aren't just taking in calories; they're absorbing the industrial waste of a broken food system. They'll continue to do so unless we actively make different choices. And the good news? We can. You don't need to eat like antiaging guru Bryan Johnson—with a spreadsheet for breakfast and a lab test for lunch—or spend a fortune to keep your kids healthy. But you do need to give a damn. Going organic is worth it. Real food, grown clean, gives your kids a fighting chance to grow up without neurotoxins hijacking their development. This approach is not about fads or labels. It's about defending your kid's health at the most basic level: their plate.

This especially applies to school lunches. I remember how shocked I was when Gretchen told me what they were feeding our kids for lunch when they were in middle school. Most of what's served in American schools is ultraprocessed garbage, loaded with refined carbs, preservatives, artificial dyes, and bottom-of-the-barrel meats that wouldn't pass inspection in half the developed world. I think prisoners eat better.

A 2021 study in JAMA Network Open found that nearly two-thirds of the calories kids eat in school come from ultraprocessed foods linked to obesity, inflammation, and poor cognitive performance. Translation? We're handing our kids toxic food on a tray and wondering why they're bouncing off the walls and can't pay attention in class. This isn't hype. It's science. And it's a call to action—your children's future health depends on it. You can start by making some simple adjustments.

Clean up the home kitchen and pack their school lunches. Don't just lead by example; remove temptation for yourself as well. When my kids were younger and started to graze like Texas cattle at my house, I made sure they'd have only healthy choices available. I'd also reward them with a special treat like ice cream or a milkshake, so they weren't totally in the "good food" bubble, but most of the time, they had no other option.

Limit the Options, Up the Intake

Before my military service, I used to wonder how people could resort to cannibalism in extreme survival situations, like in that movie *Alive*, based on the real-life story of a Uruguayan rugby team in the 1970s whose plane crashed in the desolate, snow-covered Andes Mountains. However, after being in a mock prisoner of war camp and withstanding survival training in the SEAL Teams, I understood it intimately. When you are being starved to extremes, you realize at some point you'd eat just about anything. Armed with this knowledge, I used it to my full advantage as a parent.

When my kids were preteens, I was rebuilding my lost life savings after I had shuttered my first business. I had moved to Incline Village, in north Lake Tahoe, where I was running the new digital media business I started and writing for magazines like *Maxim* and *FHM*. Lake Tahoe is a mystical place during all seasons. My kids and I have so many great memories of our time there, and we still talk about them when we all get together: skiing at Diamond Peak in the winter and spring, hiking, swimming in the crystal waters, and jumping off those big, smooth alpine rocks in the summer. These experiences were precious, and they didn't cost a whole lot of money (which was great while I was rebuilding).

In the winter and spring, I'd always get up around six in the morning before we headed to the mountain so that I had time to get ready and prepare their lunches for the day. While I tried to always make their favorite sandwiches, the sides were always super healthy. No Doritos, just carrot sticks, sliced apples, and coconut energy balls, which they still give me a hard time about.

Many of you reading along right now are probably thinking to yourselves, "But my kids are picky eaters!" Let me let you in on a little secret: *All kids are picky eaters!* Yes, getting your kids to develop healthy eating habits is one of the hardest jobs you'll have as a parent considering what you're up against. But if you are consistent and demonstrate good eating leadership yourself, it will pay off.

One of the little tricks I knew would always tip the scales in my favor was having my kids do big physical activities—skiing, hiking, swimming—to get them nice and hungry and then ambush them. I'd whip out my dad lunches to rolled eyes and a few under-the-breath grumbles like "But Daaaad, where are the Doritos?"

I'd usually reply, "As we used to say in the SEAL Teams, suck it up! You have your lunch—eat or don't eat, the choice is yours. This isn't Burger King; you can't have it your way!" Without any other food available outside of what I packed, they ate what they were given because they were starving, and there were no other options. I didn't give them much choice in the matter. Next time you do a physical activity with your kids, ensure that all the food options are healthy ones. Then watch the magic happen when there are no alternatives.

Make the Meal a Memory

Sometimes it helps to outsource the parent food preaching with great content. I used to throw on *Super Size Me* and let Morgan Spurlock scare the crap out of my kids. Nothing like watching a guy eat himself sick on McDonald's to drive home the point that what we put in our bodies actually matters. It's part documentary, part slow-motion train wreck—you can't look away, and by the end, you're swearing off quarter pounders for at least a week.

Of course, there's more to it than scaring your kids straight (though I guarantee that can help too). Instilling healthy eating habits often comes down to the special moments you create around the table, no matter the meal or where it may be. Maybe that's why *The Bear* hit so hard for me. It's one of those rare shows that fires on all cylinders: smart writing, brilliant acting, and a heartbeat you can feel through the screen. The story follows Carmy, a gifted young chef, who comes home to run his late brother's gritty, line-around-the-block Chicago sandwich shop, "The Beef."

The Bear has won a slew of Emmys, Golden Globes, Critics Choice, and other awards since its release in 2022. And though it takes place in a restaurant, the show is not really about food—it's about grief, family, pressure, and trying to hold it all together while healing old wounds. There's a moment in the show that stopped me cold: Carmy reflects on his happiest memories. They were not awards or milestones but the meals he had shared. The clatter of forks, the laughter, the comfort of sitting around a table with the people you love. It's so true when you think about it—those are the moments that anchor us.

Some of my best childhood memories are centered around meals with my family. They are a reminder of how important it is to expose our kids to special experiences, not just the big ones, but the simple, sacred ones too, like eating out together. Celebrating something special that happened. Or just finding an excuse to dress up and take your kid out for a nice dinner. You don't need to go to a fancy restaurant either. Having real conversations over real food that isn't microwaved in a rush creates memories tied to presence. Our kids should grow up knowing that life isn't just about grinding; it's about connection, being there for the people you love, and finding meaning in the ordinary moments that turn out to matter most.

Whenever I planned one-on-one trips with the kids when they were younger, I made a point of taking them somewhere new to eat, giving them the opportunity to try different places, experience different cultures, eat from different menus. At the time, it was just about sharing a good meal, doing something outside the norm, and giving them a little taste of the world. But looking back now, and after watching *The Bear*, I realize something much deeper was happening: Those meals weren't just about food; they became memories. Dad moments. It's no coincidence that Jackson lights up at the thought of sushi—it's his favorite meal we still share together—or that Madison gets excited over good Mexican food.

I remember taking Tyler out for dinner in downtown Portland, just the two of us. He'd recently moved there with his mom, siblings, and stepdad, and he was dealing with a new school, new city, new everything. He was still finding his footing. The adjustment was weighing on him, so we slipped out for dinner and ended up at this cool Thai spot in the Pearl District, the Phuket Cafe. I'm pretty sure it was T-Man's first time trying Thai food. We sat by the window, the city humming around us, and over a plate of green curry, he started to open up. He talked about feeling like the new kid, the fear of not fitting in, and the pressure of starting from scratch. We didn't solve everything that night, but we didn't need to. I listened to him, we connected, and we shared something new together.

Years later, Thai is still one of Tyler's favorite foods, and now I get why. It's not just the food he craves; it's the memory. Moments like that dinner with Tyler remind me just how quietly powerful shared experiences can be. A meal. A walk. A simple night out that becomes a lifelong memory. Like Matthew McConaughey said in one of my favorite movies, *Interstellar*, "We're just memories for our kids." And if that's true, and I believe it is, then I want to be the kind that shows up at the right moment. The one that lives in a flavor, a sound, a look across the table when the world feels too big.

Do It for Dad

As you've realized by now, I've always believed in giving kids the nudge when they need it, just enough to get them to step into the unknown, but not so much that they feel pushed off a ledge. That's where "do it for Dad" came in. It started as a playful prod, but it became a secret weapon, my nuclear option, used sparingly and only when the stakes felt personal. New food? "Come on . . . do it for Dad." Black diamond run? "You've got this, do it for Dad."

One time at my dad's (Grandpa Jack's) lake house on Priest Lake in Idaho, we'd just hiked a small trail to a secret swimming spot with a cliff jump. I went first. I looked back up and saw Madison perched at the edge of a cliff, toes curling over rock. Even from the water, I could tell her heart was pounding. I treaded water as she looked down at me, unsure. And I just smiled and said, "Come on, Maddie . . . do it for Dad." She jumped, screamed a "woohooo" midair, and splashed into the water. She came up laughing with a wide grin I'll never forget. Then I yelled at the boys to jump: "Come on, guys, your sister just jumped!"

"But she's more like you, Dad!" Jackson shouted down at me.

Madison's always had a brave streak in her, and it was a great afternoon. Oh, and the boys did eventually jump after a few more chants of "do it for Dad!"

"Do it for Dad" was never about me. It was about giving my kids the courage to try something new and scary and the story they'd carry with them afterward. They still talk about "do it for Dad." It's become our inside joke, sure, but it is also a powerful reminder of what they're truly capable of when they push past fear and lean into the unknown.

Once you've seen yourself do something hard—whether it's jumping off a cliff, trying octopus from a street cart, or simply sticking to real food and a solid night's sleep—you start to believe you can handle more than you thought. That belief begins in the body, not the brain. When we feed our kids well, help them get proper rest, and show them what it means to fuel for life, not just survive it, we give them a foundation most children never get.

Healthy food and good sleep aren't just "nice-to-haves." They're biological armor. Study after study proves that what our kids eat and how well they rest can reduce the risk of everything from ADHD to obesity, anxiety to diabetes, and even certain cancers. These aren't fringe science claims; this is hard data we've ignored for too long. By fueling their bodies with real, nutrient-dense food and protecting their sleep like the asset it is, we're helping them perform better today while stacking the odds in their favor for the next fifty years.

Field Note: Health as a Foundation

- Don't just feed—fuel. Instill family healthy eating habits with guardrails.
- Model the habits yourself. If you're crushing Doritos at midnight, your kids will too.
- Treat sleep like it's money in the bank, with the same nightly routine, including a dark bedroom and zero screens.

Family Challenge: For one week, include a plant-based protein at breakfast, take a family walk after dinner, and don't use devices before bed. See how everyone feels come Sunday.

Advice from Jackson: *Give your kids a blood test (like my dad did for me) if you want to make an impact on how important eating healthy is. I used to eat pastries every morning, but once I saw my numbers, I realized they were wrecking me. Cutting them out was way easier after that.*

Chapter Checklist

- **Don't Treat Food and Sleep like Side Quests.** Your child isn't "being difficult"—they're running on low fuel and zero rest. Like in SEAL training, performance starts with the basics. No fuel, no focus.
- **Lead by Example.** Kids follow what you do, not what you say. You can't snack like a raccoon and expect your kid to crave kale. Whether in the kitchen or at the table, show them that eating clean isn't punishment; it's power.
- **Reinforce Food as Fuel, Not a Reward.** Build the habit of explaining why certain foods matter for energy, clarity, and emotional balance, not just "because I said so." Add meaning, relevance, and value.
- **Make Healthy Food the Default.** Hungry after skiing, hiking, or sports? That's your moment. Stock up on good stuff before the hunger sets in. Starvation is your parenting ally—especially when Doritos aren't an option.
- **Pack Lunch like It's Armor.** You wouldn't send your kid to school with a broken backpack. So why send them with ultraprocessed garbage that tanks their focus and spikes their blood sugar?
- **Outsmart the System, Don't Fight It Blindly.** TikTok is selling your kid food in disguise. Teach them how to spot ads, decode fake health labels, and scroll with critical thinking. Bonus points for doing it with humor.
- **Share Meals That Matter.** Thai with your son, sushi with your daughter, a fancy dinner for no reason. New foods become new memories, and that builds both curiosity and trust.
- **Prioritize Sleep.** Sleep must be prioritized like it's life or death—because it is, emotionally and cognitively. Set real bedtimes, kill screens early, and treat sleep as essential recovery, not a bonus prize for "good" behavior.

- **Go Organic When Possible.** Cleaner food equals less poison in your kid's system. Small swaps—like milk, produce, and grains—make a big difference over time, but don't stress perfection, especially at the outset.
- **Make Meals a Sacred Pause.** Whether it's dinner out or sandwiches at the lake, create space for connection. Your kids won't remember every lesson, but they'll remember how it felt to be fully seen across the table.

6

Designing Digital Defense

We can't ask our children to disengage from screens if we're constantly plugged in ourselves. Courageous parenting starts with showing up, modeling presence, and leading by example, even when it's hard.

—BRENÉ BROWN

Research professor and bestselling author Dr. Brené Brown has become a powerful voice on vulnerability, leadership, and how we show up for the people we love. Her work has especially helped parents shift the way we think about connection. She reminds us that presence matters more than perfection, and that leadership at home starts with modeling the kind of behavior we hope to see in our kids. This mindset is crucial today as both children and adults must contend with a new enemy, one that doesn't lurk in the jungle wearing camouflage paint. This combatant pulses, flashes, and vibrates in your kid's pocket, armed with TikTok, YouTube, and Silicon Valley's finely tuned dopamine artillery.

Welcome to parenting in the digital apocalypse.

We're far past the days of yore when our ancestors faced predators in the wild. In the digital wilderness, we're dodging carefully engineered psychological bots lobbed directly into our kids' frontal cortex. Silicon Valley is the new battleground, and they don't need underground caves when they've got fiber-optic cables straight to your child's brain. Back in the SEAL Teams, we trained relentlessly for asymmetric warfare, ambushes, guerrilla tactics, covert ops. But let me tell it to you straight: Conventional parenting gets murdered in today's unconventional warfare.

Now, I'm not saying you need to rip out the Wi-Fi, bury your iPhone in the backyard, and go full *Fallout*, setting up camp in a Texas bunker with canned beans and a Geiger counter. If you haven't seen *Fallout*, it's a great show, set in a future where the surface of the Earth has been nuked into oblivion, and survivors live underground in bunkers called vaults. That is, until they're forced to enter the lawless world above.

Sound familiar? The digital world our kids are stepping into isn't that different: Misinformation, scams, fake influencers, deep fakes, online predators—they're all there, waiting to chew up the unprepared and spit them out into a digital wasteland.

If you're holding this book in one hand and your kid's digital babysitter in the other, welcome to the club. I've been there. It's way too easy to slide that iPad across the table to buy yourself just five quiet minutes. Sometimes you've got to—I get it. But let's be real: Too much screen time isn't doing them any favors. Their brains aren't built to marinate in TikTok and *Minecraft* 24/7. There's plenty of research backing that up, some of which is detailed in this chapter, but honestly, you don't need a study to tell you what you already know: Hand a kid a tablet for too long and it's like trying to have a conversation with a zombie that only speaks *Fortnite*.

According to Common Sense Media's 2023 census, kids aged eight through twelve are clocking nearly six hours a day of non-school screen time. Still tempted to shrug it off? Here's your ice-water bath, courtesy of cold, hard science (no fluffy pseudoscience here): A 2023 *Journal of Psychiatric Research* study dropped some napalm-grade findings from a massive survey of over 100,000 American kids. Excessive screen time comes with the following:

- Higher ADHD risks
- Learning delays
- Speech impediments

- Conduct disorders (translation: kids acting like tiny digital warlords)
- Early autism spectrum behaviors

Watching YouTube Shorts isn't just harmless scrolling; it's a neurological carpet-bombing run. And Silicon Valley's dopamine pushers will continue rewiring our kids' brains one TikTok dance at a time if we let them.

But you are not helpless. Just like I hammered home in my book *Mastering Fear*, awareness isn't paralysis—it's your rallying cry. You need to build a digital perimeter, SEAL sniper style: disciplined, structured, and ready to eventually hand off the responsibility to your kids. They are inevitably going to have as much access to the internet as they want, so before that happens, it's important to talk with them, teach them the dangers, and set them up to make their own successful decisions.

Major Digital Challenges

There are four major challenges we're up against as parents in the digital age:

1. **Screen Time.** Managing the amount and quality of time children spend on digital devices.
2. **Social Media.** Steering children clear of addictive, anxiety-inducing social platforms.
3. **Digital Scammers and Predators.** Protecting children from online threats that can lead to financial loss or exploitation.
4. **Exposure to Harmful Content.** Shielding children from inappropriate material, including pornography and dark web content.

Let's consider each one in turn.

Screen Time

Scrolling through your phone at dinner? Not a good idea. We have to lead from the front, as always. In the SEAL Teams, we call this exemplary leadership, and it is so incredibly important to raising our kids. Exemplary leadership—exhibiting the behavior we want to see reflected by our children—requires parental commitment; in this case, we cannot prioritize our phones over our loved ones.

It's not easy for us parents, especially with how fast technology is developing. You can safely assume your kids will be running your household IT by the time they turn ten. My kids are Gen Z to the bone—the first fully digitized generation, raised by glowing screens and silicon-chip babysitters. And somehow, despite TikTok's dopamine drip and YouTube rabbit holes, I survived parenting them without descending into madness, at least mostly. You're likely in the same boat, but you also have the additional concern of artificial intelligence to deal with these days.

I still laugh when I think back to when my youngest, Tyler, stared at me at age seven, baffled, blurting out, "Dad, what the heck is a CD?" It was like looking into the innocent eyes of an early man encountering fire for the first time. If that doesn't officially stamp "digital dinosaur" on your forehead, nothing will. So brace yourself: Your offspring will inevitably outrun you technologically by the third grade, turning you into an obsolete, thumb-fumbling relic overnight.

Gretchen and I smugly believed we were ahead of the digital curve until our eldest, Jackson, turned eleven and immersed himself in computers, Python code, *Minecraft*, and AI. Just to give you a little taste of what we were up against, when Jackson turned twelve, he wrote a program that crawled government open-source databases. Just input your name and social security number, and the program would find out if the government owed you any money. He ran our whole family through the program, and it turned out the State of California owed his grandmother (my mom) $12,000 in some unclaimed tax overpayment from the sale of an old house.

Jackson called his grandma, affectionately known as "Neema," to explain where to claim the money. A few weeks later, a check arrived from the state's comptroller. My mom couldn't believe it! (Neither could I.) She paid Jackson a $500 commission. We were all in shock. And suddenly, Gretchen and I realized we were less "tech-savvy parents" and more like the clueless early hominids gawking at that black monolith in Kubrick's *2001: A Space Odyssey*, grunting and scratching our heads in primitive bewilderment. By the time Jackson started hammering out Python code, we at least felt relieved that we'd instilled solid boundaries around screen time and taught him the difference between good digital decisions and online dumpster fires.

But if we hadn't instilled those boundaries and led by example, Jackson's tech experience may have gone south fast, and it could have affected him for the rest of his life. Let me drop the polite act for a moment: If you spend dinner scrolling through Instagram or compulsively checking work emails, don't be surprised when your kid's attention span shortens to that of a New York alley cat. Kids mimic what they see—this is monkey-see, monkey-do psychology 101—and as a parent, your first job is to quit preaching about screen time and start modeling the behavior you expect.

This idea of leadership by example isn't some cheesy, self-help nonsense—it's the SEAL way. In the Teams, there was no "Do as I say, not as I do" BS allowed; it was always "Do exactly as I do, because the opposite gets people killed." Parenting doesn't have the same immediate mortality rate (thank God), but it shares the same principle: If you're zoned out, half-assed, and digitally addicted, you're training your kids to follow suit.

Social Media

Social media is like a digital narcotic, and we're quick to hand it to our kids like candy—especially here in the US. Kids get full access, no watchdogs, and digital predators and algorithms are hunting for fresh prey around the clock. Compare that to China's approach, and it puts us to shame: Anyone under fourteen gets just forty minutes a day of screen time, blocked entirely between 10 p.m. and 6 a.m., and all their access is tied to real-name IDs to enforce age limits.

I'm not antitech. Hell, I run businesses and publish content across platforms daily. But giving a twelve-year-old unrestricted access to Instagram is like dropping a frag grenade in their emotional development and hoping for the best. In a 2023 study published in *JAMA Pediatrics*, researchers found that kids who spent over three hours a day on social media had *double* the risk of developing symptoms of anxiety and depression. That's not "maybe it's bad"—that's a red flare firing straight into your parenting foxhole.

The same people who design slot machines in Vegas engineer the social media dopamine loops; only now they've figured out how to make us all chase likes instead of a cash payout. It's a trillion-dollar industry designed to hijack attention, wreck confidence, and rewire kids' brains before they're even fully formed. In business terms, for kids, social media is mostly downside with very little upside.

In our house, we held the line against social media until ninth grade, and even then, we kept it tight. If you're on the fence about letting your seventh grader get Snapchat because "everyone else has it," here's my advice: no. You're not here to win a popularity contest; you're here to raise healthy kids, not approval junkies. You wouldn't let your kid roam a nightclub at midnight with a fake ID, so why let them loose in the digital sewer?

If you can manage it, keep them off social media until they're adults. If I could rewind the clock, I'd push my kids' exposure back to eighteen years old—high school graduation age—when they'd at least had the opportunity to build real-world confidence and some scar tissue. I wish I'd tried harder on this one, and hopefully you can accomplish it. The reality is, you'll likely have to use some parental persuasion to get them to buy into a plan of "no social media until adulthood." Think of something fantastic you can trade them in return for staying out of the social media gutter: maybe a bucket list trip with their friends or a car, a big reward that holds true value to them, though that doesn't necessarily mean expensive. We have to be practical and realize that all humans are creatures of habit—sometimes positive incentives work best to condition our kids.

At sixteen, our oldest, Jackson, feeling the anxiety and pressure that comes with being on social media, decided on his own to delete all of his accounts. I can't tell you how proud this made me. His younger siblings have socials, but luckily, they aren't very active, which we're thankful for.

Digital Scammers and Predators

Online scammers? Been there, done that, and the risk for kids is real. Consider these findings: 79 percent of young people aged eight to seventeen encounter online scams at least monthly, with 20 percent being exposed to scams online every day. Alarmingly, online scams have affected nearly half (46 percent) of this population, and 9 percent have lost money to these scams. In fact, according to a study from Stanford University, teens and kids are getting hammered by online financial scams. Between 2017 and 2022, money lost by US youth under twenty spiked by a mind-blowing 2,500 percent. That's not a glitch in the system, that's a digital ambush. And our kids are walking straight into it.

Our first taste of online scams aimed at our children happened one afternoon when Jackson was about nine years old, playing games on his grandmother's computer. Suddenly, a pop-up ad lit the screen like a Vegas slot machine: "Congratulations! You've won a FREE iPad!" All he had to do was enter a credit card number to cover shipping.

"Grandma, I won!" he shouted, eyes wide, heart pounding.

She hurried over, both of them caught in the high of digital confetti and too-good-to-be-true excitement. Credit card in hand, they started typing, visions of shiny tech glory dancing in their heads. Then Gretchen walked into the room. Eyebrows raised. Instincts firing.

"What's going on?" she asked.

"Mom, I won a free iPad! Grandma's helping me pay for shipping!"

Gretchen didn't hesitate. "Stop. It's a scam."

That one moment, seconds away from handing over financial information to some online fraudster, was a gut check. If his mom hadn't been there to spot it, Jackson and his grandma would've learned that lesson the hard way. Mom for the save, again.

The digital world isn't a playground—it's a battlefield. And as parents, we have to give our kids digital body armor. Like the saying goes, knowledge is power. After that near-miss with the "free iPad," we sat all the kids down—Jackson, Madison, and Tyler—and had a serious talk about the online scams. Not a fear-based lecture, but a full-on mission briefing. We laid it out plainly: Scams aren't just something that happens to "other people." They're targeted; they're sneaky; they're everywhere. And if you're not paying attention, they'll catch you slipping before you even know what hit you.

We talked about some of the obvious red flags: phishing emails, shady pop-ups, and why anything that starts with "Congratulations!" and ends with "Enter your credit card" is probably a message aimed at ripping you off. Every parent needs to have this talk, and earlier rather than later. Walk your kids through examples. Show them screenshots of scams. Let them see how easy it is to fake a life online with rented supercars, Photoshop abs, and paid-for followers. Break it all down before someone else sells them a dream that costs them their trust, their money, or worse, their dignity.

Now that AI can clone your voice with a small voice sample, consider creating a secret family code word as well. Keep this simple and make it easy to remember for your kids. Remind them that any serious request coming their way claiming to be from their parents or other family members needs validation with the family code word. For example, if your child gets a call that sounds exactly like you asking them to meet someone outside, they'll know to ask for the family code word, and if it's missing, they will hang up and call you directly.

When I talk about awareness, I'm not talking about paranoia; I'm talking about paying attention to the world as it really is. It's a lesson I learned young, in one of those moments that brands itself into your memory. Let me take you back to a rainy morning in Birch Bay, Washington. My sister and I stood at the bus stop, rain jackets zipped, backpacks dripping. I was in third grade, she was in first. Our mom had just dropped us off and was a tiny yellow speck in the distance, driving away in her VW Beetle. That's when a strange man pulled up in a sedan and leaned out the window. He smiled and said our parents had asked him to give us a ride to school.

Even as a kid, something about him didn't feel right. My sister froze. We both remembered the rule our mom drilled into us: Never get into a stranger's car, no exceptions, and if it's ever real, they'll know the family code word. He didn't. I didn't have to ask; I just knew.

Here's the wild part. My mom said later that halfway down the road, she felt something, a tingling feeling only mothers know, a sense of dread. She slammed on the brakes, spun the wheel around, and came roaring back toward us. She pulled up just in time to see the man notice her car and speed off in a panic. That season, there had been a string of kidnappings in the area. We weren't one of them because my mom trusted her instincts, and she'd taught us to trust ours.

That lesson stuck. Awareness isn't fear; it's power. Whether it's a stranger at a rainy bus stop or a message in your kid's inbox, the rule is the same. Prepare your kids before the world tests them. Teach them what to look for, what to do, and that their safety is never negotiable.

Kids are curious. They're wired to explore. But curiosity needs a compass. Your kids need to be digitally street-smart the moment they get online; think of it like the digital version of teaching them to wait for the light and look both ways when crossing the street.

Thankfully, Jackson's story had a soft landing. Grandma's card never got charged, and my son learned a lesson without getting burned. But it could've been bad. Let this be your reminder: The internet is not neutral ground. Equip your kids as you'd equip them for a mission. Because out there, things can go sideways fast.

Another dark digital reality you can't afford to tiptoe around is online predators, those twisted creepers lurking behind fake profiles and friendly avatars, hunting your kids like wolves circling a fresh kill. Think I'm exaggerating? The National Center for Missing & Exploited Children reported a nearly 35 percent jump from the prior year in online child exploitation reports in 2022 alone, totaling over thirty-two million incidents. That's roughly 88,000 cases—and thousands of digital predators actively stalking our kids—every single day. If you aren't teaching your kids how to navigate this threat, someone else online will be eager to step in, and it sure as hell won't be someone you trust.

In early May 2025, the FBI deployed fifty-five different field offices in lockstep over five days to dismantle a nationwide online predator network. The result? 205 offenders in cuffs, and 115 kids rescued from digital enticement, trafficking, and distribution. Most alarming was that this was no "creepy guy in the basement" takedown: Among the traffickers nabbed was a Minnesota state trooper *in uniform*, a DC cop, a priest, and other community leaders—all "trusted adults" who preyed on the vulnerable.

Just as you need to discuss digital scams with your kids, you need to talk to them about online predators because, like it or not, they will pop up, even in places you'd assume were safe and family friendly. Thankfully, we never experienced that nightmare ourselves, but that was luck, not strategy. If I had a do-over, I would have started these talks as early as seven years old, right when kids first start dipping their toes into the potentially murky internet waters. Explain that not everyone online is who they say they are, and some people may pretend to be kids or "friends" just to trick them.

Kids don't need fearmongering either—they need straight talk, examples they can recognize, and permission to press the eject button without guilt. Give them clear, simple rules:

- Never share personal information like their full name, school, or home address.
- Never agree to meet someone in person who they only know online.
- If anyone makes them uncomfortable, tells them to keep a "secret," or pressures them to do something, they should stop immediately and come straight to you.

When you have the talk, drive the point home. Doing memory exercises in sniper school, I learned that most people need a graphic, shocking image to cement something into their memory. So I recommend getting real. Share true stories of kids getting stalked online and the consequences that followed. Get graphic, if necessary, in order to drill it into their heads.

Exposure to Harmful Content

All right, time to rip the Band-Aid off. Let's talk about the one topic most parents would rather jump from an airplane with no parachute than confront: online porn.

Before I get to our story, it's important to understand that the internet isn't just YouTube and homework sites. There are entire digital back alleys—places like 4chan, Reddit's darker corners, and other anonymous forums—where kids can stumble across toxic content and graphic porn or even be targeted by predators. These spaces thrive on shock value, secrecy, and zero accountability, which makes them dangerous for young, curious minds that don't yet know how to filter what they're seeing.

Now buckle up. This one's not for the faint of heart. A 2023 study revealed that 40 percent of fourth-grade boys actively search for pornography online, and their parents have no clue about what they are up to. Our first experience with the issue was with our oldest, and it caught us both off guard. When Jackson was around eleven, Gretchen called me, mortified, after stumbling onto anime porn she found in his browser history. Not wanting to scar the kid with maternal shame, she tossed this digital grenade straight into my lap. Later that day, after Jackson got home from school, I called him privately and dropped a white-lie bomb. "Listen, buddy, when we gave you your computer, we put some spy-grade monitoring software on it. I got pinged about some anime cartoon stuff—you and I both know exactly what I'm talking about. Let's keep this minor incident off your mom's radar, but please steer clear of this stuff from now on, got it?"

Yes, this "software" was total bullshit, but it was also effective. I didn't have to be there to know he turned pale, relief washing over him when he realized Mom was staying blissfully unaware. "Yes, Dad, sorry, Dad, just curious," he stammered quickly.

I reassured him, "Hey, I get it. Just use better judgment next time." Clearly, he'd sent out a sibling-wide alert about Dad's "spyware," because that was our first and final porn-related incident in the household. There would be more serious stuff to deal with later on, but for now, mission accomplished.

In hindsight, we should have had a conversation about online pornography and more before Jackson became curious. As certified sex therapist Emily Jamea, PhD, explains, "They are going, at some point, to stumble across something on the internet that they are not prepared for or don't really understand." That's not pessimism—that's reality. Research from the American Academy of Pediatrics finds that the average age of the first exposure to online pornography is now around eleven, and a 2023 Common Sense Media report found that most parents underestimate how often kids encounter sexual content online.

It would have been much better to have the talk openly and tell Jackson what our expectations were for him: to make moral decisions, to understand that intimacy and sex aren't what's portrayed in those videos, and to avoid looking at content that sends the wrong lessons. The conversation doesn't have to be graphic or clinical. It can be as simple as "You're going to see things online someday that show sex in ways that are unhealthy or unrealistic. When that happens, I want you to come to me, no shame, no punishment. We'll talk about it honestly, and I'll help you understand what's real and what's not."

What the research makes clear is this: If parents don't talk about it, the internet will. And the internet doesn't care if your kid is ready for the conversation.

Set Digital Rules

Kids are sharp, sometimes scary sharp. They'll out-GPT you, out-hack you, and find the loophole in your rules before you've finished your first cup of coffee. But there's a catch: Raw intelligence without guidance doesn't build character, it just builds clever manipulators, the Jeffrey Epsteins or Elizabeth Holmeses of the world. That's why we parents can't just be spectators. We have to step in, lay the groundwork, and lead with clarity.

To that end, we need to reinforce right and wrong, whether online or in everyday "real" life. Not just once, but repeatedly, in ways that make sense to our kids' brains at their stage of development. Because sometimes, they genuinely don't know the difference.

Other times, they know, but the temptation to "get away with it" overrides their moral compass.

For example, Tyler, like his dad, has always been extremely creative with his financial side hustles. I experienced this for the first time while I was living in Puerto Rico. I left him and his older brother Jackson alone in Old San Juan for a few days when I had to fly to New York to take care of some business. Jackson had just turned eighteen. Tyler was fourteen.

What could go wrong?

I called to check in that first night I was away, and Jackson said Tyler had earned a hundred dollars on the basketball court.

Oh, this has gotta be good.

There's a nice outdoor basketball court that overlooks the warm Puerto Rican ocean in the "La Perla" neighborhood, which was about five minutes from my house at the time. The thing about La Perla is that it's a rough part of town after the sun goes down. Turns out Tyler had been shooting hoops on the lighted court after dark when he met a drunk rapper and his crew who saw Tyler draining threes and challenged him to a shoot-off for twenty dollars.

Tyler accepted, of course—only he didn't have a penny to his name. Thankfully, the kid has game, and he ended up taking a hundred dollars off this guy. Nobody was the wiser. But this could have gone terribly wrong.

Now that you have a little background, let me explain what happened with eighth-grade Tyler and his foray into his own online scam. Tyler had been buying and reselling sneaker drops and got scammed on PayPal with a clawback payment from a buyer. This opened his eyes up to scams and gave him a blueprint on how to run his own. (Gotta appreciate the hustle!)

He discovered he could fraudulently obtain sneakers from StockX. In his mind, this was a genius life hack. He got the shoes, the money back, and a story to tell. And honestly, part of me admired the creativity and tactical thinking. He'd identified a loophole and executed like a miniature con man. But that's fraud; it's illegal, and more importantly, it's wrong.

So I had a talk with him, not in anger, but with clarity. I walked him through the real-world consequences. What seems like a clever hustle when you're fourteen becomes a criminal record when you're eighteen. I also explained that real money doesn't come from "flipping" sneakers on StockX or any seemingly "legitimate" scam, like get-rich-quick crypto gurus. It comes from a good plan, hard work, consistency, and discipline.

It's our job as parents not just to punish but to teach and to explain that integrity matters even when nobody's watching—even when you could get away with something. Because the habits our kids build now are the foundation of the person they'll be when life gets harder and the stakes get higher. We need to help them see the line but also understand it—not just where it is but why it matters. And as uncomfortable as it might feel, these are exactly the talks we have to have, especially in a world that constantly, especially in our politics, blurs right and wrong in favor of "whatever works."

So what did the Webb crew do in our modern family household to tackle these digital land mines and challenges? We kept it simple. I'm a big believer in the military principle of KISS: Keep It Simple, Stupid. It's saved lives in combat, and believe it or not, it works in parenting too. Complexity kills momentum, especially in a household full of kids bouncing between school, sports, and modern life's digital madness.

What follows are the core ground rules that worked for us. We didn't lift them from a parenting guru's blog, and maybe they weren't perfect, but they were clear, practical, and achievable. Most importantly, we stuck to them. Before you discuss any of the topics covered in this chapter with your children, first sit down with your partner, talk it out, and create your own KISS-based rules of engagement. Make them useful. Make them realistic. And for the love of all that's sacred in the parenting trenches, model them.

Because your kids are always watching, even when you think they're just scrolling TikTok. And long after they forget what you said, they'll remember what you did:

- No cell phone until age thirteen
- No social media until high school (as mentioned, I'd consider no social media at all until eighteen, but you'll have to reward your kids with something in return)
- No devices at mealtime (we allowed them to read a book if they were bored while we were out)
- No screens after 8 p.m.

These rules weren't just practical; they were personal. I created boundaries I knew I could hold myself to as well because after years in the military, I understood one truth better than most: You can't lead from behind. If I wanted my kids to take these rules seriously, I had to live them first. They had to see them. Feel them. Watch me walk the same line I was asking them to follow.

The digital world isn't just noisy; it's a minefield, and it is only ramping up. The best we can do as parents is not to try to rewind to some presmartphone utopia; it's to adapt, to own the terrain, and to build a family code that fits the world we're living in right now. We can't pretend it's 1985 and hope screen time just goes away. We must guide our kids through the digital war zone. Because if we're not leading them, someone else will. The algorithms and influencers are waiting to take our place, and they don't give a crap about our kids' character, confidence, or well-being.

You don't need to be a tech expert; you just need to have a plan. Don't be afraid to get some help either. High school kids are great for this job—you can hire a young tech whiz to help you set parental controls and keep you up to date on sites and material to avoid, whether 4chan or the dark web. Our kids' minds are the high ground, and if we don't hold it, TikTok and the AI dopamine dealers may take our places. So step up. Set the standard. And show them how it's done. Draw your line. Set the rules. Be the example. And when in doubt, remember: You're not raising followers, you're raising leaders.

Field Note: Own the Digital Feed

- Model the focus you want them to keep. If you scroll at the table, they will too—kids imitate what they see.
- Build digital perimeter lines. Device-free meals, no screens in bedrooms, and agreed-upon shutdown times.
- Train attention like a muscle. Small bursts of undistracted reading, building, or creating will grow their focus over time.

Family Challenge: Establish a daily 30-minute device-free block for the whole house. Hold the line.

Advice from Jackson: *Make sure your kids learn math, physics, and how to code. These skills are just as necessary in today's world of artificial intelligence as learning to read was a hundred years ago.*

Chapter Checklist

- **Get Real with Your Kids.** Talk with them early on about digital scams, online pornography, the dark web, 4chan, 8kun, the Tor browser, and the dangers of online predators. Make them digitally street-smart so they avoid the shadowy digital alleyways.
- **Restrict Access.** Do not allow them to use messaging apps like Telegram and Signal, which are used by criminals.
- **Do Not Allow Devices at Mealtime.** This should include when eating out at a restaurant. Sometimes kids find adult conversations boring, understandably, so don't be afraid to let your kids read at the table sometimes. This is a practical compromise (and there's no study I know of that says reading is bad for kids!).
- **Wait for Phones Until Age Thirteen.** Studies show early smartphone ownership (under age thirteen) correlates with higher anxiety, sleep disruption, and reduced face-to-face social skills. At a certain point, though, having a phone is practical and a great safety tool for tracking and communicating with your kids.
- **Create Parental Controls.** Unless you're homeschooling your children, they are going to get computer exposure starting around kindergarten, so it's best to have someone who is IT savvy to help you set up search and access parameters on the devices your kids might use.
- **Shut Down at Night.** Don't allow screen time after 8 p.m. Research shows that kids with screens in their bedrooms sleep one hour less on average and report more behavioral problems than those who don't.

7

Talking About Sex, Drugs, and Alcohol

I can resist everything except temptation.

—OSCAR WILDE

Here's a stat that should make every parent sit up straight: According to the CDC's Youth Risk Behavior Survey, by age thirteen, nearly one in two American kids have already been exposed to pornography. By senior year of high school, over 50 percent have tried alcohol, and more than 40 percent report having had sex. These aren't college kids. They're your seventh graders, your freshmen, the kid whose laundry you still fold.

We want to believe our children are innocent, shielded, and safe, but the truth? They're swimming in a culture that doesn't wait for permission. TikTok, YouTube, and Snapchat aren't just apps; they're full-time influencers shaping your kid's view of sex, drugs, alcohol, money, and identity before you even get a word in.

Adolescent boys are especially difficult during their developmental years. According to a study from the American Academy of Pediatrics, boys' brains show heightened reward sensitivity and lower impulse control during adolescence, making them more likely to resist authority and test limits. They are wired for risk-taking and independence, and pushing boundaries is part of how they figure out who they are. That's biology, and good luck trying to fight it.

Instead of pretending sex isn't happening, drugs don't exist, or every kid waits until they're twenty-one to have their first drink, honesty, openness, and real conversations are the best way to approach these topics when your kids are old enough to grasp them. Too often, parents clamp down with shame and secrecy, like you unfortunately see in a lot of American households, especially around sex.

And yet, there's a paradox here. Sometimes a white lie is the right tool. Telling your five-year-old that the dentist's drill "just tickles a little" is better than winding them up with a play-by-play of what's coming. Pretending Santa exists for a while? That's not deception; that's magic. Those little lies protect innocence, buy trust, and give kids the confidence to step into new experiences without fear.

But when it comes to the big stuff—life-shaping, identity-shaping, soul-shaping knowledge and experiences—our kids deserve the truth. They deserve to know that alcohol isn't just "something adults do"—it's a risk; sex isn't just "something for later"—it's about responsibility and respect for another person. Kids are smarter than we give them credit for, and when we dodge the truth to "protect" them, we don't shield them; we just end up leaving them unprepared.

I'm a Taylor Swift fan, and she puts it perfectly: "No matter what happens in life, be good to people. Being good to people is a wonderful legacy to leave behind." Truth telling is part of that goodness. Our honesty, even when it's messy, is the legacy that shapes how our kids will make their own choices.

Research backs this up. Not just what we say—but where we say it—matters. A 2024 study led by Dr. Dina Izenstark at the University of Illinois found that parents and kids communicate more openly when they're side-by-side—in the car, on a walk, or doing something together—rather than sitting face-to-face. Those shoulder-to-shoulder moments take the pressure off, lowering defenses and turning hard talks about sex, drugs, or relationships into conversations instead of confrontations. Skip the kitchen-table stare down. Talk while you drive, walk, or cook dinner. Sometimes the best parenting happens in motion. If we clamp down too hard during the teen years, we don't just risk rebellion; we risk losing the connection that makes parenting work. Teenagers need room to stretch, to screw up, and to find their footing while knowing we're still in their corner. That's the tightrope we walk as parents, holding the line without pulling it so tight they break away. The goal isn't control, it's trust. When we stay steady, even through the awkward, uncomfortable talks, we're showing them what calm leadership looks like. And that's what sticks.

I want to pull back the curtain on how Gretchen and I navigated the high school gauntlet—sex, drugs, and rock 'n' roll (well, mostly alcohol)—and all that comes with raising kids straddling the line between teenager and adult, without losing them in the process.

Let's start with the three-letter four-letter word: sex.

Honest Discussions About Sex, Relationships, and Gender

When it came time, I was grateful that Gretchen took the lead with Madison; thank God for her wisdom and steady hand. With the boys, the responsibility landed on me. I didn't sugarcoat it. The last thing I wanted was for them to learn about sex from YouTube or in the locker room, so I gave it to them straight.

Being a good observer—maybe it's the sniper in me—I figured out that my sons had seen just about everything in the book when it came to the act of sex. Boys in my generation would sneak a look at a *Playboy* magazine, but now? Hell, there are whole Reddit forums that would humble a sex addict. Trust me, they've likely seen it all, so I decided to just talk to them about general respect for the opposite sex, sexual partners, responsibility, consent, and safe sex. After "the talk," there's not much more you can do other than let your kids do what they're going to do. Hopefully, they'll be responsible about it and come to you if they need help.

Gretchen and I definitely took a more European style of parenting when it came to sex, and it worked for us. In the US, too often sex gets treated like this forbidden, off-limits topic until kids are already deep into figuring it out on their own, usually through what they pick up online (and it might shock you at what's out there). However, in much of Europe, especially countries like the Netherlands and Sweden, parents talk openly with their teens about sex early and often. They focus on education, responsibility, and healthy relationships rather than fear or punishment.

According to the *Journal of Adolescent Health*, American teens are more likely to experience unintended pregnancies and sexually transmitted infections compared to their European peers—who have more honest conversations around sex—largely because of differences in parental communication and comprehensive sex education. By normalizing the conversation at home, we gave our kids the knowledge, respect, and trust to make smarter choices, without the awkwardness or rebellion that comes from making sex feel taboo.

What has always struck me as backward is how in American culture, sex gets treated like something that must be hidden from kids, talked about only in a whisper, while violence is blasted across every screen every day as if it's no big deal. We'll let a ten-year-old watch people get blown apart in a movie—guns blazing, blood, guts, and bodies flying—but God forbid there's a scene with actual nudity. That's somehow off-limits.

It's a shame, and it's one of the big things we need to improve on as a culture here in America. When you treat sex like something dirty or forbidden, kids don't stop being curious; they just learn to figure it out in all the wrong places: quietly, online, through peers, or through trial and error, without real guidance. Meanwhile, instead of connection or responsibility, violence is normalized. That's a dangerous trade-off if you ask me.

Keep the Lines of Communication Open

Jackson was the first to dip his toe in the water. He had two serious girlfriends at different times in high school, and like most young men learning to navigate love, heartbreak, and growing up, I'm sure he crossed the line into intimacy with both. But it was his senior year when we had a moment that stuck with me. He was dating a girl I'll call Kristin. She was smart and funny, and together the two of them looked like they belonged in some indie coming-of-age movie.

I had a loft in the Pearl District in Portland back then, right next to REI downtown. When I wasn't using the condo for work trips or visits with the kids, I'd rent it out on Airbnb. Jackson had a key to check up on the place when I wasn't around. It didn't take a detective or a dad's intuition to figure out he'd probably been using it as his own little getaway spot with Kristin, a safe place where they could have some freedom. And honestly, I was fine with it. By that point, I trusted him to make smart decisions, and I figured it was part of growing up.

Like most high school relationships, though, it eventually ended. I don't know exactly how it fell apart—probably like most young love does—but I know it was Jackson who pulled the plug. And that's when things took a turn I didn't see coming.

Out of nowhere, Jackson received an intense, blindsiding email from Kristin's mother. This wasn't simply a concerned-parent note; it was a full-on character assassination. She accused Jackson of being emotionally manipulative and wrote things about me and his mom that were flat-out false and way over the line. But what shook me wasn't just what she said; it was that she sent it directly to him. Seventeen years old, just figuring out life, and now he's got an adult unloading her own emotional issues on him through email with zero warning.

Jackson was rattled. I could hear it in his voice when he called me to speak about it. And here's the part that hit me hardest: He came to me and asked if I'd help pay for him to talk to a psychologist about what had happened. Seventeen, proud, independent, and he still had the trust in me to say, "Dad, I need a little backup here." I didn't hesitate. I said yes right away.

That moment says more about what kind of relationship we'd built than anything else. I wasn't controlling his choices; I was just being steady for him when things got heavy. If we hadn't established open communication early on, he may have never come to me. I also knew my limitations as a parent. As much as we want to believe we can handle everything ourselves when it comes to our children, sometimes the strongest move is knowing when to bring in outside professional help.

Jackson and I were sitting at our regular Sunday dinner recently, talking about this book, and out of nowhere, he said, "Dad, I'm really grateful you said yes to that. It meant a lot that I could lean on you with no judgment." That's the kind of thing that stays with you—not just that he needed help but that he trusted me enough to ask for it.

Show Them They Matter

If you're lucky enough to have a son and a daughter, then you know how different they are, especially when it comes to the relationship between a daughter and her father. When Madison was born, I began learning about how much of a daughter's sense of self-worth—and even her expectations in future relationships—are tied directly to how her father treated her growing up. I read a ton on this topic as a young dad. I had heard about its importance, but it wasn't until I started looking further into it that I realized just how much research is out there about it.

So if you have a daughter, pay attention.

A study published in the *Journal of Family Psychology* found that daughters who reported having a strong, positive relationship with their fathers were more likely to form healthy romantic relationships as adults. Fathers set the standard for what kind of love and respect they believe they deserve. When I read this study for the first time, it felt like a blast of air from a C-130 ramp lowering for a skydive.

From then on, I made it a personal mission to show Madison exactly how much she mattered not just as my daughter but as a young woman becoming her own person. Her mom and I didn't want to turn her into a bridezilla or inflate her ego in a way that wouldn't serve her. But I was intentional about treating her like she was a queen, whether taking her out to nice dinners one-on-one, introducing her to strong female mentors I knew from my professional groups like YPO or the Entrepreneurs' Organization, or just reminding her that she deserved real respect. Those weren't just dad moments; they were building blocks for the kind of future I wanted her to have: Confident. Independent. Knowing her value before anyone else tried to define it for her.

I remember my guy friends who'd comment about how I had my hands full with such a beautiful daughter, but I knew Madison was raised well by her mom and me and was perfectly capable of making her own solid decisions. This is why I wasn't worried about her choice of boyfriends. By the time Madison was in high school and started showing an interest in dating, I wasn't pacing the floor at night or sighting in my rifle at the firing range like some overprotective-dad stereotype. I was confident her mom and I had done the work early, building her self-worth, teaching her what respect looks like, and giving her the tools to figure it out on her own. Sure, I heard from her siblings that there were a few of those "cool guy" types along the way, guys who probably cared more about showing off than showing up. And yeah, I'm sure some of them burned her. But even those hard lessons are part of the process. You can't shield them from every disappointment, but you can raise them strong enough to walk away from it unscathed. And that is Madison—she's a strong one.

Eventually, she found her first real, serious boyfriend, Jason. I remember meeting him for the first time and how nervous he was to meet "the dad." I took Jackson, Tyler, Madison, and Jason out for burgers and could tell by the lack of eye contact that Jason was super nervous. So I said, "Jason, what are you so nervous about? I can only kill you with my bare hands!" Jackson and Tyler started to crack up, Jason turned white, and Madison screamed, "Daaaad, stop it!"

Sometimes it's OK to have a little fun with the boyfriend.

In all seriousness, as a dad, there's no better feeling than knowing your daughter has chosen someone solid, and I could tell that Jason was a good kid. He came from a great family too, which makes all the difference. Even though Madison and Jason broke up later on, in their first year of college (he had followed her to London to study), it says everything about the kind of people they both are that Jason's parents are still close to Madison and our family. Sometimes we bump into them on our travels and catch up over dinner. It always feels like we are old friends rather than exes' parents. That's when you know you raised a daughter who not only picks good people but also becomes one herself.

Parenting in the New Gender Landscape

Just as we need to be real about sex, romance, and relationships, we've also got to recognize another evolving part of parenting in this generation: gender identity. Now, I've never personally dealt with gender identity questions in my own kids, but I've had close friends walk that path with their children. For example, one close friend shared how their child came out to him and his wife as nonbinary. What inspired me was how they handled the situation with love and respect. There was no judgment, no trying to change them. Just pure unconditional love and support. They found a therapist. They listened. They gave their kid space to feel safe, seen, and loved. And that should be our default mode as parents—all we can do sometimes is to just show our children love and support.

Look, I'm a straight-shooting former Navy SEAL who grew up in the '80s, when this kind of thing wasn't just ignored—it didn't even exist in popular conversation. But parenting isn't about preserving the past; it's about preparing our kids for their future. And I've got to say, I'm proud of how my Gen Z kids and their friends are handling this new terrain. Their emotional intelligence around gender, identity, and inclusion is next level. They're not just checking boxes on tolerance; they're showing up with empathy, curiosity, and real backbone. They're teaching me a thing or two about what it means to lead with love, not fear.

Your kid doesn't need you to be an expert in gender theory. They need to know that if they're ever confused, scared, or questioning who they are, they can come to you, that there's no version of themselves that could make you shut the door. Because that's the job—love them hard. Love them through it and through everything else. And let your presence be the safe harbor they can always return to. That doesn't mean shielding them from every tough moment or trying to control every decision. It means walking beside them as they navigate those moments and supporting them no matter what.

Keeping It Real About Drugs and Alcohol

It may come as no surprise that the drinking and drug scene is alive and well at any campus near you—from the stories I've overheard, most of these kids would give Keith Richards a run for his money. But what might be a bit more shocking is how many kids are exposed to drugs and alcohol long before they head off to college. A government-sponsored national survey on drug use and health found that roughly one in three twelfth-graders reported using illicit drugs in the past year, and almost half have tried alcohol in the same time frame. Close to one in ten teens experiment with harder drugs like cocaine or ecstasy, even those whose parents thought they were "responsible" kids. And when teens see substance use normalized among friends, their own risk skyrockets—almost one in five cite peer pressure as their main reason for trying drugs.

Let's be honest, whether you think your kid's school or social circle is "safe" or not, they're going to run into drugs at some point. I learned pretty quickly that no bubble can keep them fully insulated (as you may recall from "Operation Weed" in chapter 3). And if you think they're sheltered at some fancy private school, think again: Based on my experience with my YPO friends—whose kids attend some of the best private schools in the country—they're probably more at risk. But there are some steps to take to help your kids navigate these tricky waters. Just like with sex, it starts with open, honest conversation.

Presence and Straight Talk

The very first time I heard my kids joking about their school's party scene, I didn't ignore it. I didn't pretend it was a phase. I said, "If you want to talk about it, I'm here." No judgment, just straight talk. Science backs up this approach: Effective parental involvement, being present, and keeping open lines of communication seriously lower the chances of early drug use. In fact, a 2012 study published in the *Journal of Adolescent Health* found that adolescents who reported strong parental monitoring and open communication were significantly less likely to engage in early substance use compared to peers who lacked that involvement. As a family, we discussed the downsides of drug and alcohol abuse—more than once—and I used real-world examples whenever possible to drive the point home about the dangers.

The one story I shared with all my kids was about one of my best friends growing up, Joe, a story that's stuck with me my whole life. Joe was like a brother to me as a young teen in Ventura. We surfed, skated, and worked on the same dive boat—together almost all the time. But everything changed in my senior year of high school when I noticed Joe and our friends who hung out at the harbor were starting to go down a dark path.

I was seventeen, and I'd just come off a multiday trip working as a deckhand on the dive boat *PEACE*. I met up with Joe and my usual group of friends at the Italian restaurant in the harbor right above where the boat docked. Skateboards under our arms, it felt just like any other night. Back then, it was the usual: some forty-ounce beers, a little weed, nothing I hadn't seen before. But that night was different. We stopped at one of those grimy harbor bathrooms, and I watched, for the first time, Joe and one of my other friends pull out a homemade rig and start freebasing cocaine right then and there. Joe looked at me and casually offered it my way, like it was no big deal. I told him no. But what affected me the most wasn't that moment—it was what happened after.

A few hours later, when the high wore off, I watched those same guys—guys I'd grown up with—go back to that same filthy bathroom, trying to scrape up some leftover resin like full-blown junkies. Their faces, their eyes, they weren't my friends anymore. They reminded me of that nasty little creature Gollum, who was obsessed with the ring of power in *The Lord of the Rings*, one of my favorite book series.

That was the first time I saw the raw grip of addiction right up close. I wasn't some innocent kid by then; I knew what partying looked like, but this felt different—this was different. It was utter desperation, and it scared the shit out of me. That night, standing under those cheap yellow lights in the harbor, I made a decision: I needed to get the hell out of there. I needed a new environment, or I'd end up exactly where they were. That's the night I knew I had to join the Navy.

Years later, my mom called me up when I was a new SEAL on Team 3. She told me she had been in the parking lot at Whole Foods in Ventura when some homeless guy with no teeth started yelling her name. "'Lynn!'" she said, "I thought, how the heck does this man even know me?" Then she realized—it was Joe. The same Joe who'd been in that bathroom. The same Joe who didn't make it out.

By the time I was preparing for my Navy career, Joe was already slipping into full-blown meth addiction. I wrote about this in my memoir, *The Red Circle*: Watching Joe unravel scared me straight. I remember seeing him months later, completely spun out, pupils like dinner plates, mumbling things that didn't make sense. The same guy I used to skateboard, surf, and dive with was now a ghost in his own skin, with yellowing teeth and breath that could peel paint off a concrete wall.

I didn't pull any punches when I talked to my kids about drugs. I'd tell them, "Let me paint you a picture of how fast things can go bad." And that's the story I'd lay out for them, especially when we talked about the difference between experimentation and getting caught in something you can't pull yourself out of. I never wanted them to live scared, but I did want them to live aware. Because that's the truth about hard drugs: They don't take long, and they don't care how smart or tough you think you are. They'll gut your life from the inside out before you even see it coming.

Unfortunately, I'm sure almost everyone reading this book has had a "Joe" at one time or another in their life. Don't let your kids repeat their mistakes. Tell them the story, share those experiences. Joe's story is why those conversations mattered so much to me as a parent. Relaying it to my kids wasn't about controlling them; it was about passing on a hard-earned lesson, hoping they would never have to learn it the way I did. Having these conversations is as important as doing your best to ensure your kids are in the right kind of environments, activities, and friend groups in school. If you do your job right up to that point, the rest is honestly up to them. We have to trust them to make good decisions. But we can also give them real-world tools to make smart choices in the heat of the moment.

No-Questions-Asked Help

One rule I laid down with all my kids was the no-questions-asked Uber ride home. I told them flat out, "I don't care if you're drunk, high, or just feeling sketchy about a situation, call me or order the ride. I'll pay for it—no lecture, no guilt trip, even if it's three hundred bucks at two in the morning." I'd rather eat that bill than get the call no parent ever wants. I'd personally seen a car full of high school seniors lose their lives during grad week my senior year at Nordhoff High School, and I didn't want my kids anywhere near that kind of situation. This rule built a safety net they knew they could count on when things got real. At the end of the day, I'd rather have them home safe than sitting somewhere making a decision they can't take back.

De-Risk Exposure

A study published in the *Journal of Adolescent Health* found that students involved in team sports were significantly less likely to engage in substance abuse, especially alcohol and marijuana use. This is another reason I think it's great to encourage kids to do sports or activities that elevate their peer groups and essentially de-risk their exposure to the normalization of illicit drug use. As you know by now, Jackson and his sister were on the speech and debate team, Madison also competed on the ski team, and Tyler focused on basketball and golf in high school. Any structured activity—especially team sports or performance-based clubs—that gets them moving, collaborating, and focused on goals is a win. The structure, accountability, and sense of belonging that come from being part of a team or club create a protective buffer against risky behavior. So yeah, keeping your kids busy in all the right ways? That's not just good parenting—it's prevention.

Steering Through the Chaos

I'm not here to scare you into bunker mode, but we need to understand that our kids are going to experiment. Whether it's alcohol, sex, or testing limits in some way, most will try *something* risky by the time they graduate. According to the CDC's Youth Risk Behavior Survey, over 50 percent of high schoolers have tried alcohol, and about 40 percent report having had sexual intercourse by their senior year. But teens who have open communication with their parents are significantly less likely to engage in high-risk behavior. One major study from the *Journal of Adolescent Health* found that teens with supportive, involved parents were more likely to delay risky behaviors and better equipped to make safer choices when they did decide to engage. I think the best we can do is to raise them so they are equipped to make their own choices and then hope they choose well.

Our job isn't to eliminate the risk. We can't. But we can reduce the fallout. We do that by staying connected, asking real, relevant questions, and making sure they know they have a lifeline when they need one. And here's the truth: Most of the questions parents ask are total bullshit. "How was your day?" "Did you learn anything?" "Everything good?" These aren't conversation starters; they're check-the-box scripts, and your kid knows it. These questions don't open doors; they shut them.

If you want real answers from your kids, ask better questions. Try "What was the weirdest thing you saw today?" or "Who made you laugh?" or "Did anything happen that made you uncomfortable?" Questions like these peel back the layers. They signal to your kid that you're not just checking in; you're curious about them, and you're paying attention. Open communication, honest curiosity, and presence—those are the tools that help kids steer through the chaos and come out stronger on the other side.

The high school years can especially feel like a war zone: sex, drugs, and booze, it's all coming at them (and you) fast. But it doesn't have to be a battlefield. It can be a launchpad. When we stop trying to control every move and instead focus on guiding, listening, and setting honest, firm boundaries, something powerful happens. Our teens start to rise. They fall at times, sure, but they also get back up and make that ascent. The goal isn't to raise perfect kids. It's to raise young adults who know how to stand back up, who aren't afraid to question the world, and who still see you as a safe place to land time and again. Give them space. Give them truth. And above all, give them love and support that doesn't flinch when things get messy.

Field Note: Keep the Mic Open

- Trust doesn't grow from lectures; it grows from open dialogue, especially about the messy stuff.
- Go first. Share a real story from your own life and the lesson you learned. Sharing your own vulnerability cracks the door open for them to do the same.
- Ask better questions. Skip the yes/no traps. Try "What are the pressures your friends are dealing with in school now?" instead of "Are you doing this?"

Family Challenge: Run a "20-minute no-judgment talk" this week. One tough topic. Your job: 80 percent listening, 20 percent talking.

Advice from Tyler: *Give your kids space to figure things out. Let them try, fail, and make their own calls. That's how they grow. But when things get hard, be the parent who shows up.*

Chapter Checklist

- **Talk Early, Talk Often.** Normalize real conversations around sex, relationships, consent, drugs, and alcohol before the world gets to them first. Share your own life experiences and mistakes to build connection and credibility.
- **Don't Wait for a "Right Time."** Start the uncomfortable conversations before an emergency arises.
- **Ditch the Scripted Questions.** Skip "How was your day?" Ask "What made you laugh today?" or "What's something weird that happened?"
- **Define Your Family Values.** Be clear about your expectations while leaving room for your teen to explore and ask questions.
- **Make Space, Not Shame.** Teenagers need autonomy and support, not punishment masked as discipline.
- **Take a European Lens.** Treat sex like something to be respected and discussed—not hidden or feared.
- **Assume They'll Experiment.** Focus on harm reduction and open-door policies instead of rigid control.
- **Establish Lifeline Rules.** Offer a no-questions-asked Uber ride policy or late-night call clause for emergencies.
- **Be the Safe Place.** Remind them often: "No matter what happens, you can come to me."
- **Stay Curious, Not Controlling.** Teens will shut down if they sense judgment—ask, listen, and breathe.
- **Teach Them How to Handle Pressure.** Talk about peer influence, digital exposure, and what to do when things get real.
- **Keep Them Engaged.** Sports, clubs, side hustles, and structure equals safety; activity reduces risk.

8

Creating the Forever Family

The strength of the team is each individual member. The strength of each member is the team.

—PHIL JACKSON

Phil Jackson is widely regarded as the most successful coach in NBA history. He won eleven NBA championships as a head coach, six with Michael Jordan and the Chicago Bulls and five with Kobe Bryant and the Los Angeles Lakers. But what set him apart wasn't his playbook alone—it was his mindset. Jackson brought Zen philosophy, Native American teachings, and a deep respect for individual growth into the locker room. He coached legends, but more importantly, he helped them become better teammates, leaders, and men. Jackson understood what every parent should tattoo on their soul: Life isn't won by lone wolves—it's a team game.

One thing I swore I'd do better than my parents? Play life as a team and keep the family intact. I've thought long and hard about that idea, watching America slowly turn the family unit into a fractured relic, like rotary phones or Blockbuster. In America, nearly one in four adults reports feeling estranged from at least one family member. According to Cornell University's Family Estrangement Project, 27 percent of families experience some form of long-term disconnect. That's not just sad; it's a cultural epidemic.

In other parts of the world, that kind of estrangement would be unthinkable. In many Asian cultures, elders aren't seen as burdens—they're viewed as anchors. In countries like Japan, China, South Korea, and Vietnam, there's a deeply rooted respect for the elderly that's built into the social fabric. Parents care for children, and later, children care for parents. It's not considered optional or sentimental; it's duty, legacy, and pride rolled into one forever family.

Housing arrangements are just the start. In such cultures, decisions are often made with multiple generations in mind. Grandparents play an active role in raising grandkids, and family wealth and responsibility are shared. Further, aging isn't hidden or feared—it's honored. Compare that to the US, where "independence" gets pushed so hard it often turns into isolation. We send aging parents to senior homes and wonder why our kids stop calling.

We have to reimagine the American family unit for ourselves because it's as lost as a blind man in the woods. It's up for reinvention, and it starts with you and me to make that happen. I'm not saying every other culture has it figured out, but there's something to be learned from societies that treat family as a lifelong, evolving team, not a temporary project that ends when the kids move out. That's the model I'm trying to build with my children. Longevity. A family that sticks together, grows together, and when the time comes, is there for each other. I never wanted to be some ghost dad whose kids ship him off to a retirement home with peeling wallpaper and nurses who confuse morphine with pudding. No thanks. I wanted to build something that lasts, something worth coming back to.

My own playbook for family wasn't written on a clean slate. Like a lot of lessons we learn in life, it came from watching what not to do. As you've picked up on by now, my dad and I have carried a complicated history, which includes a decades-long tug-of-war over "truth." For years, I tried to mend fences, but we always seemed to get stuck—him holding tight to his memories, me holding tight to mine. He's got his stack of diaries and receipts; I've got fragments—some sharp, some hazy—the confused recollections of a teenage kid attempting to make sense of it all, and later, the reflections of a thirty-year-old Navy SEAL trying to manage loss, war, divorce, parenthood, and the transition back to civilian life.

For a long time, the love between my dad and me got buried under misunderstanding, pride, and unspoken pain. But here's what matters now: We've recently taken a positive step. My dad agreed to joint counseling, and for the first time in decades, it feels like there's room for healing. Proof that keeping a positive outlook—even after thirty years of missteps—can still pay off.

I don't share this to criticize him. There are just as many good memories as hard ones, and there's a lot I admire about my dad. What I've learned through our relationship is this: Ego and score-keeping will bleed a family dry. And trying to "win" the past is the quickest way to lose your kids in the present. Like my good friend and New York restaurateur John Bush says, "To have good friends, you gotta be a good friend." I think the same applies to parenting. To have good kids, you've got to be a good parent. That means letting go of the scoreboard, owning your mistakes, and choosing love over being right.

I went over the edge of that father-son war, and the view on the way down wasn't pretty. But falling taught me something: You can't build a forever family on bitterness and scorecards. You build it by breaking patterns. By saying, "Yeah, my parents screwed some things up, and so will I, but the buck stops here. I'm going to learn from this and raise my kids with more grace than I got or gave."

That became my vow.

Here's the part that gives me hope: My kids already get along in a way I never experienced growing up. My sister, whom I love deeply and respect for all she's achieved, never shared that easy bond with me after I left home at sixteen. We've managed to coexist as adults, but it's never been effortless. Watching my kids laugh, fight, and still come back to each other is living proof that the cycle can be broken.

When I saw how naturally my kids clicked with each other, I knew I had to learn from my own past, protect that, and build on it. I wanted to create an environment that not only kept that bond strong but made them want to keep returning for birthdays, for holidays, for no reason at all. A place where the door is always open, the laughs come easy, and the family feels like a crew you'd actually choose. That's the long game I'm playing. And so far, it's working.

That said, it's not always easy. As your kids start entering adulthood, there are big conversations to be had, whether about money or picking colleges, before they flee the nest. And even if they're gone, off living their own lives, you'll need to build a home base so strong and welcoming that they will want to come back again and again. Giving them a safe place to turn, a refuge from the rest of the world, is part and parcel of a forever family, a family Phil Jackson would be proud of—one that stays together, not out of obligation, but out of love.

Shift from Command to Counsel

Once the Friday night lights dim and the cap-and-gown photos are snapped, that's when the real questions start creeping in for our kids: Who the hell am I? What do I actually want? Where am I headed? The singer Katie Pruitt nails this sentiment in her song "Expectations." Pruitt sings about all the things they don't bother to teach us in school, the real-life obstacles, like how to navigate identity, pressure, heartbreak, and the weight of everyone else's opinions:

All those years of bad test scores
Still trying to figure out what I was studying for
But once you walk out that classroom door
Nobody tells you where you're going
Seems like everyone I know
Is just an actor putting on a show
I hope one day I'm wise enough to know
That there's no way of knowing

I love that song—so many hard truths in those lyrics.

Nobody hands out a syllabus or a cheat sheet for adulthood. If you're not careful, you could end up living by the script the world wrote for you instead of writing your own. This is why I told my kids to carefully choose what gives them energy and attention in life. If our kids waste their energy chasing approval, they'll run out of it before they ever get to chase their own purpose.

When that moment came for my children, I made one thing clear: Chase your damn passion. I didn't care if it led to a university lecture hall, a welding apprenticeship, or backpacking through Southeast Asia with a beat-up journal and a questionable haircut. I wasn't about to cram them into a mold. I'm glad they all picked the college route, but I never pushed it like some suburban script. The military gave me discipline, direction, and a front-row seat to life's harshest truths. But that was my path. College, trade school, gap year, whatever it may be, it's all about getting out of the nest and learning how to flap your own wings. I told them, "Find your fire, follow it hard, and don't expect a damn map. Just go."

And most importantly: "I'll be here if you need me."

In the high school years, I started consciously shifting from command to counsel around the time my kids turned sixteen. Maybe it's because I was on my own at that age, but I deeply believe in giving them the wheel around then, letting them start to make their own choices, and allowing them to learn from the consequences.

Yes, it tightened my chest when they began making real-life decisions around relationships, sex, college, and hard truths, but I knew it was time to loosen my grip. That's when all the character, discipline, and values we've helped them build either hold or crack. We lead them when they're young so that they can lead themselves as they get older. And while we're still there, if they hit rough waters, the purpose of the shift from command to counsel is to let them decide for themselves, live with the consequences, and grow.

A 2024 study in *Frontiers in Psychology* found that autonomy-supportive parenting—stepping back while staying engaged and available—is linked to higher motivation, stronger self-control, and better academic performance in teenagers. An analysis of thirty-six studies showed that such an approach consistently leads to healthier adolescent development as well, including psychological resilience and improved attitudes toward school. To put that simply: When we shift from commanding to counseling—trusting their judgment while guiding from the background—we're setting them up to handle life on their own terms, with confidence and character. And this was how their mom and I handled their high school years. It wasn't perfect, but we survived! Which brings me to a family minefield to navigate together: money.

Dopamine, Debit Cards, and Dollars

If you think hormones are intense, wait until your teenager gets their first taste of swiping a debit card. In high school, the "I wants" hit like a dopamine freight train: designer clothes, trendy sneakers, upgraded phones, nights out with friends, travel, the list goes on. That's exactly why these years are the perfect time to start talking seriously about money, spending, and financial literacy, before their first real paycheck or their first credit card becomes an expensive life lesson (recall Jackson's "little" financial faux pas in chapter 2).

Having a real conversation with your high schooler about money might feel strange or uncomfortable, but it's one of the smartest moves you can make as a parent. These discussions give them context around your family's financial reality, especially if your house isn't run by a magic ATM that never runs out of cash. The earlier they understand that resources are limited, the less likely they are to treat you like their personal bank.

Now, you can preach to them all day about smart spending, but I've learned with teens and young adults that external validation lands differently. When teens enter that glorious phase where they think they know more than you—probably because they've grown up with the internet in their pocket—what you tell them may not sink in without a little help. "Why listen to Mom or Dad when I can watch some finance 'genius' on TikTok?" So teach them the basics, but also point them to smart, validated podcasts, books, and YouTube channels that reinforce the financial wisdom you're trying to pass down. Often, the same truth just needs a new voice.

Teaching Money Before Money Teaches Them

I'm still floored that most schools don't teach the difference between good debt and bad debt. Instead, they send our kids off to college with zero financial training, then let the credit card companies set up shop outside the dorms like loan sharks at a pool party. It's predatory. They know Mom and Dad will bail Junior out after he maxes out a card on spring break in Panama City.

In talking to other parents in my network, I've found we're all over the map when it comes to supporting our kids financially. Some hand out cash like it's candy at Halloween, others cut their kids off completely at a certain age. I've always tried to land somewhere in the middle. My philosophy has been, I'll give you what you need, but you're going to work for the rest. Like Warren Buffett famously said, "Leave your children enough so that they can do anything, but not so much that they can do nothing." I've also always tried to be transparent with my kids about my financial situation to expose them to life's financial realities. For example, I wanted them to see how I juggled the cost of college for three kids without turning into a stressed-out mess.

When Jackson and Madison were in high school, they got partial allowances because they were hustling. Madison had her sneaker art and a vintage clothing business. Jackson helped me out with my business, but he also did some tech gigs—he came to find that there's decent money in helping Boomers back up their iCloud and organize their digital disarray. One of the guys Jackson helped—an ex-Goldman banker and great friend of mine—ended up investing in his start-up. It's amazing what happens when kids prove themselves to the right people.

Then there was Tyler.

Tyler got a full allowance—not because he was lazy, but because his hustle would've likely landed him in juvie.

One afternoon, I got a call from Jackson while he was still at St. Andrews. "Dad," he said, "Tyler's being entrepreneurial, like you, but maybe a little too entrepreneurial. He's selling something not *quite* legal. I talked to him, and if you offer an allowance, he'll stop."

Tyler had a booming gummy business—not the vitamin kind. I wasn't mad. In fact, I was impressed with the initiative, just not the product line. I didn't want to blow up the trust Jackson had built by intervening too harshly. So I called Tyler and kept it simple: "Time to retire the gummies, focus on school and sports. I'll set you up with an allowance if you can agree to focusing on your school and helping your mom and stepdad around the house."

We even drafted a contract: GPA requirements, sports involvement, no drugs or alcohol (ironic, I know), and bonuses for making varsity and academic performance.

This is what I sent him back in 2021:

Tyler,

Your mom and I are very proud of you and want the best for you.

We love you very much and want you to be the best you possible. Everyone has their different skills and passions and we are excited that you have your own. Your mom and I want to support your love of sports, and talent on and off the court/field in every way we can.

If you agree to the below contract we can start your allowance today.

Tyler agrees to maintain the following:
—3.0 GPA
—Be involved on sports teams year round (travel or high school).
—Help mom and Bob [Tyler's stepdad] when asked and be respectful to house rules.
—No trouble at school or outside of school.
—No drugs or alcohol (as an athlete you need to eat healthy and take care of your body).

Allowance
$75 per week ($150 paid 1st and 15th)

Bonus
GPA (bonus of $200 for 3.0–3.5 GPA. 3.6–4.0 is $400). Bonus is paid for each grade reporting period.
$200 Bonus for making Varsity team (any sport). Bonus is paid each year you make varsity and upon completion of season. You have to finish season for bonus.

If any condition is not met then allowance for that month is forfeited and mom and I will determine with you what's best beyond that but we know you can achieve this and be your best you.

Please reply all that you agree.

Love you,
Dad

And it worked—again proof that humans respond well to performance incentives!

Set—and Keep—Boundaries

Once my kids started high school, they began noticing that Dad was doing better financially. Dinners got fancier. Trips to Europe replaced the local beach in Tahoe. But I was clear with them: Just because life looked cushy didn't mean there was unlimited access to the vault. One instance stands out. We left my apartment in New York and headed to my home in Puerto Rico. I'd been upgraded to business class on Delta using points, and the kids were stuck in economy. Cue the grumbling. I turned around and said, "When you earn your own money, you can fly whatever class you want." That shut it down fast.

I wasn't trying to be cold; I was trying to teach them something that most kids never learn: Gratitude and drive are built when you understand the difference between what's earned and what's given. I continued to tell all three of them that I'd pay for college, and even housing and food. But the fun stuff? That's on them. If they wanted bar tabs, music festivals, or midnight sushi runs, they had to get a jay-oh-be.

I even gave them options: Find your own gig or help me run one of my self-storage investments as the site manager. As discussed in chapter 2, Jackson did an amazing job as a site manager, modernizing so much of what we did. Then he dug into P&L and tax strategy. One day, he looked at me, seemingly annoyed, and asked, "Why don't they teach this stuff in school?" That frustration led to something bigger. He saw firsthand how the leading, but outdated, storage software was lacking in basic features, so he built LandLord while in college (with a little help from Dad). That spark started with managing one dusty Florida facility in the middle of COVID.

Here's the story he tells in his company website's "About" section:

> When I was 17, I bought my first self-storage facility with my Dad.

> The problem? I was still in high-school. As the manager, I was taking calls, moving in and out tenants, auctioning late tenants, tracking accounting, and more while trying to get my home work done.
>
> It was all too much, so I coded my own tools to automate the self storage facility so I would have time for homework, finding a date to the prom, and managing the facility.
>
> This automation brought the facility's occupancy from 60% to 92% in 3 months, and two years later I learned the value of automation. In 2020, I sold my facility for $500,000 profit to a new owner who was thrilled that it was completely automated.
>
> I put those same tools into Landlord so any self storage owner can use them. Most Landlord customers make 8.5% more revenue in the first year and only spend a few hours a week managing their property.

Watching that idea go from frustration to solution was a proud dad moment.

Meanwhile, Madison took on the second facility we bought in the Carolinas. She wasn't naturally drawn to the storage business like her brother, but she gave it her all. She learned to file taxes, handle angry late-paying tenants, and juggle real-world responsibilities while still a college freshman.

I remember the first time she came face-to-face with adult life there. "Dad," she said to me one day, "this guy told me he would pay his rent three times and never did. Do people actually lie about this stuff?"

"Yes, they do, Maddie," I replied.

"OK, got it," she said.

I think that was her first online unit auction.

Those lessons—grit, communication, accountability, and real life smacking you upside the head—aren't taught in classrooms; they can't be. And as she steps into a career in industrial design, I know she'll bring all that with her.

I never set out to turn my kids into mini moguls. But I did want to give them opportunities to learn about how money works and how work works. And yes, every one of them had to read Robert Kiyosaki's *Rich Dad, Poor Dad*—required reading in the Webb household. Because the truth is, if you don't teach your kids about money, someone else will—and that someone might be Visa.

The Launching Pad

As my kids were finishing high school, we naturally started talking about where they wanted to go to college. In chapter 4, I write about how we made goal-setting a family ritual. That tradition wasn't just about chasing grades or hobbies; it was about planting the seeds for long-term vision. By the time my kids reached junior year, we had already built that foundation, and they were used to thinking in terms of goals and direction. So when the time came to talk about life after high school, we were able to have honest conversations without any pressure.

I floated the idea of military academies, but I got shot down like a Russian drone over Ukraine. This comes with the territory when your dad's a former Navy SEAL.

Well, I had to try!

I even pitched the Coast Guard Academy to Tyler, but nada. Not one of them was interested. And honestly, that's OK by me—I just wanted them to understand all their options. They didn't need to follow my path; they needed to think about their own. They knew I expected them to at least have a rough plan of what came next. College became the direction for all three, and what mattered most to me was that they chose it themselves.

College Advisers

If your kids (not you) choose college, I recommend getting them a college adviser. Especially as a parent who didn't go the traditional college route, an adviser was super helpful. For undergrad, I had gone to night school while I was a sniper instructor in the Navy, so navigating today's complex admissions world wasn't exactly second nature. Having someone in our corner who understood the process made a big difference.

You don't need to shell out thousands for private consultants. There are incredible free college advising programs out there for families. Organizations like College Advising Corps, CollegePoint, uAspire, and QuestBridge offer one-on-one help, often virtually, to guide students through applications, essays, financial aid, and scholarship matching. Even tools like BigFuture by College Board and ScholarMatch offer structured support and are loaded with helpful content. If your school district hosts college nights or guidance counselor workshops, take full advantage. These resources are out there, and if you lean into them early, you'll save your kid, and yourself, a lot of stress down the line.

When I got Jackson a college adviser, however, I became increasingly frustrated with what the US college system had turned into—less meritocracy and more box checking. After all the work Jackson had put into high school—maintaining a 4.3 GPA, becoming an Academic All-American in speech and debate, and nearly acing the ACT—I was stunned when his adviser said he didn't have much of a chance of getting into MIT or Stanford, two schools he was interested in. On top of that, I was already disillusioned by the skyrocketing cost of college in the US and how easily the system could be manipulated. (You may have seen that Netflix documentary *Operation Varsity Blues*, where ultrawealthy parents pay test takers, bribe coaches, and create fake resumes to get their kids into prestigious schools—eye-opening and infuriating.) This frustration was what first got us looking across the Atlantic.

School on the Other Side of the Pond

When I first looked into the UK and European university systems, I was blown away. The education was world-class, and the admissions felt more merit based. As for the cost? A fraction of what you'd pay in the States. This opened up a whole new world for our family. In the US, even a public university can easily run $25,000–$40,000 per year when factoring in tuition, housing, books, and fees. Private schools? You're looking at $70,000–$90,000 annually, and that's before student loan interest kicks in. In contrast, top-tier universities in the UK and Europe offer internationally respected degrees at a much more reasonable price.

Take University College London (UCL), King's College, or the University of Edinburgh, some of the best in the world. Tuition for international students averages around £20,000–£25,000 per year (about $25,000–$32,000), and the programs are often three years instead of four, which means you're out the door faster and with less debt. Madison attended Goldsmiths at a total cost of less than one year at a US private college. In places like Germany or the Netherlands, you'll find high-quality English-taught bachelor's and master's programs where tuition can be as low as €3,000–€4,000 (around $3,500–$4,600) a year, and in some cases, free.

Bottom line? The international path is not only doable—it's smart. It allowed us to take a global view on education and gave my kids exposure to other cultures, systems, and ways of thinking that they couldn't have gotten stateside. Still, Tyler stayed closer, attending the University of Oregon, and we couldn't be happier.

Let's take a quick look at how college played out for each of my kids. I've shared where they landed, but the bigger story is in the how and why—and where they're headed now. My hope is that by pulling back the curtain a bit, you'll see ways to guide your own kids through this same process.

Jackson and St. Andrews

Jackson graduated from high school in the middle of COVID, and man, what a wild ride that was. I'll never forget sitting through that "drive-thru" graduation on Zoom. It was like ordering a milestone from a fast-food window. No packed gym, no cap toss, no senior prom. Just a screen, a few honks, and the weirdness of trying to celebrate a rite of passage during a global lockdown.

After that, I started running the numbers: Three kids heading off to college in the US, and the price tag was enough to make even a former Navy sniper flinch. Again, we're talking $60,000 to $80,000 a year per kid. Multiply that by four years, and you're looking at $240,000 to $320,000 per child. For three kids? That's somewhere between $720,000 and nearly a million dollars just to get them across the graduation stage. That kind of money isn't a simple line item; it's a financial kidney punch that makes you question whether you're funding higher education or buying a seat on Jeff Bezos' next rocket to space.

Gretchen was incredibly supportive when I brought up the idea of looking at schools overseas. It would've been easy to shut it down out of fear or unfamiliarity, but instead, she leaned in with curiosity and an open mind. She wanted what was best for the kids, even if it meant exploring uncharted territory. That kind of partnership made all the difference, and I'm grateful for it.

Of course, once we started looking at international schools for Jackson, the peanut gallery came alive. Suddenly, every grandparent had an opinion. "Why not an American university?" "Is it safe over there?" "Don't they drive on the wrong side of the road?" The group chat lit up like Times Square on New Year's Eve. That's when I decided to cut through the noise and drop this gem: "Great! If anyone wants to pitch in some cash, you can absolutely have a vote." Let's just say it got real quiet after that. Radio silence. Funny how fast strong opinions disappear when there's a price tag attached.

So it was decided that Jackson would apply to schools in the UK. His first choice was Imperial College London, one of the best in the world for computer science. But thanks to pandemic delays, his final math scores weren't released in time to meet the UK admissions deadlines. That shut the door on Imperial, but another one opened. He pivoted to his backup: the University of St. Andrews in Scotland. Looking back, it was a blessing in disguise.

The experience turned out to be nothing short of magical. He thrived there, both academically and personally, surrounded by historic architecture, world-class faculty, and a tight-knit international student body. Gretchen also loved the choice—her mom was a Scottish immigrant, so in some ways, it felt like a homecoming for the family. St. Andrews gave Jackson the education he wanted and the cultural roots he never expected.

Jackson graduated from St. Andrews on a warm, breezy Scottish summer morning in 2024, and we all made the trip. His mom, Madison, Tyler, and I all packed into the tiny, charming town on the eastern coast of Scotland to celebrate his achievement. If you don't know St. Andrews, it's the same school where Prince William met Kate Middleton, and it has the idyllic feel you'd expect for a place that would host royalty.

The school itself looked like it had been plucked straight from the set of a Harry Potter film. Madison turned to me at one point, with a smirk, and said, "So when do they pass out the wands, Dad?" That line pretty much summed up the magic of it all. Walking through the cobbled streets and stone buildings, you could feel the history humming in the air—not just the university's, but our family's as well. It was surreal watching my son—whom I once had to bribe to eat his broccoli—cross the stage at one of the oldest and most prestigious universities in the world. His mom and I were both tearing up when Jackson walked onto the main stage to accept his diploma from the dean. We'd been through so much as a family: war, going broke, losing friends, divorce, and all the battles of parenting in between. It was one of those rare full-circle parenting moments, the kind that sticks with you forever.

Madison and Goldsmiths

A few years later, it was Madison's turn. She cast a wide net, applying to her top picks across both the US and UK. Scholarship offers came in from heavy hitters like NYU and Parsons, and while those were exciting, the sticker shock was insane. Even with $100,000-plus in scholarships, it was still more affordable to send her to one of the most prestigious art schools in the world. She also got into Central Saint Martins, but Goldsmiths won her over.

Thanks to her International Baccalaureate (IB) school credits, she skipped the first year and graduated with honors in just three years. Her mom couldn't make it to London for her big graduation design show, but Jackson and I attended. We gave Gretchen a full report with photos, videos, and FaceTime calls. Madison's thesis and exhibit were based on how to use natural swamp filtration to clean industrial waste and color textile fabric in the filtration process itself. She comanaged the show as a student leader and wrote a lot of material in the brochure and signage. I was so proud of her.

Now Madison's at the Royal College of Art finishing her master's degree, arguably one of the best art schools on the planet. Not bad for a kid who used to paint custom sneakers in her mom's garage.

Tyler and the University of Oregon

Tyler is always quietly watching, taking mental notes. Just like his siblings, when it came time to choose his path, he made a bold move of his own. He's always been the black sheep of his siblings, and I love this about him.

Tyler set his sights on studying finance at the University of Oregon, and from the jump, he made it clear he was following in the family tradition of charting his own course. After seeing how much

Jackson and Madison grew from their time abroad, he told me flat out, "I want that same experience." So he's already planning a year in Madrid, ready to soak in everything from the language to the culture to the global perspective.

When we had that discussion, it was one of those moments as a dad where I felt both proud and damn grateful. He's sharp, driven, and wired a lot like me—curious, a little rebellious, and always learning by doing. And since he's a die-hard sports fan, Oregon's energy is going to fit him like a glove. He's going to have a blast, and more importantly, he's going to grow.

Seeing Tyler chart his course reminded me that sending your kids off isn't the end of parenting—it's just the start of a new position on the team.

Be the Captain They Still Want to Sail With

There's a myth out there that once your kids leave the house, your job's done. Like you pack them up, wave from the porch, and cross parenting off your to-do list. I never bought into that idea. The role doesn't end at eighteen; it evolves. You shift from household commander to coach, from full-time captain to trusted adviser.

That shift meant sitting each of my kids down—Jackson first, then Madison, then Tyler—for a real talk. I told them, "Your mom and I did our best. We're not perfect. You're old enough now to see the dings and dents in the hull. Own it, learn from it, and don't waste time blaming the past." Because now it's their turn at the wheel.

I have spent a lot of time thinking about what kind of relationship I want to have with my kids moving forward. I took notes from my parents, and from Gretchen's folks too, on what worked and what didn't. For me, it came down to this:

Be the captain they still want to sail with.

Friendly, steady, always at the helm. I'll laugh with them, share stories, and pour a drink. But when the weather turns, I steer. I don't unload my panic. I don't ask them to carry the weight. That's not their job; as parents, it's ours, and it always will be if we do it right. If you've come this far, you're on the right course.

Even when they're grown, they still want to look up to us. Maybe they won't say it out loud, but they're watching. They always are. And that fuels me. I don't have to be perfect, but I want to be worth their respect. I've seen what happens when that admiration crumbles. When the pedestal breaks and parents fall off, it's hard. But it's not about staying on top, it's about staying solid. Real. Dependable.

That belief shapes everything for me, right down to where I live. I chose Lisbon, Portugal, as my home base because it's easy to reach, and I've got enough beds to house a small battalion. I wanted it to feel effortless to visit Dad, not like a logistical headache. My goal is simple: When my kids think of a break, I want my place to be first on their list.

When they come to visit, I go all in. Stocked fridge, beach time, father-daughter mani-pedis, outdoor movies at Blackcat Cinema, and whatever turns a regular visit into "We've gotta do that again." It's not about showing off, it's about showing up in a way that makes them want to keep coming back. (This also means making sure they know their friends are always welcome.)

I've seen so many parents retire somewhere remote, then wonder why the grandkids never visit. A postcard view won't beat three layovers and bad Wi-Fi. I didn't want my house to be a shrine. I wanted it to be a magnet. A place where everyone feels welcome. A home that's still home, even when they've built one of their own.

This is my playbook for the next chapter in my life as the father of adults: Lead like a captain, love them madly, and create experiences that keep them tethered to home, wherever that may be.

Because the story keeps going. Every late-night talk, every hard decision, every small act of presence adds up, and we can always learn from our kids just as much as they learn from us.

That's what I hope for you, too—not to follow my playbook to a T, but to write your own. With effort. With love. With just enough self-awareness to grow alongside your kids, not above them. Parenting is about raising good humans, but it is also about keeping them close, creating the kind of family that lasts, not out of obligation, but out of connection. Because in the end, the real measure of parenting isn't just raising kids who can stand on their own—it's raising kids who still choose to stand with you.

Field Note: Let Them Soar

- Launch them with roots and wings: values they can stand on, relationships they can stay in, skills that let them soar.
- Keep showing up. Calls, visits, and help when they ask for it, respecting their independence.
- Traditions matter. Shared rituals keep the center strong when miles grow long.

Family Challenge: Create one new family ritual your grown (or soon-to-be-grown) kids can count on monthly.

Advice from Madison: *Say "I trust you" more often. It matters, especially when we're not sure we trust ourselves yet.*

Chapter Checklist

- **Shift from Command to Counsel Around Age Sixteen.** Trust them to take the wheel while staying available.
- **Be Clear About Financial Support.** Provide what they need; let them earn the rest.
- **Teach Financial Literacy Early.** Budgets, debt, investing, and the value of work are rarely taught at an early enough age—make it a priority.
- **Give Them Real-World Responsibility.** Help them find part-time work, get them to manage a project, teach them to file taxes.
- **Keep Them Coming Back.** Retire someplace easy to get to. Stock the fridge, invite their friends, and make it feel like home.
- **Start Family Traditions That Outlast the School Years.** Foster annual trips, rituals, and reunions.
- **Build a Family Brand.** Make them proud to rep your family crew.
- **Be the Captain They Still Want to Sail With**: Remain calm, wise, and always in their corner.
- **Lead by Example.** Show what growth looks like even in adulthood.
- **Raise Puddle Jumpers.** That's what it's all about: raising resilient, brave humans who leap, learn, and keep coming back.

Conclusion

At the start of BUD/S Hell Week during SEAL training, they marched us to the edge of the Pacific in the pitch black. The gut check? A two-mile swim into the dark, with nothing but a faint light on a bobbing safety boat in the distance. No pep talks, just a gravel-throated voice growling, "That's the turnaround. Get moving." And so we swam, half frozen, half broken, already wrecked from weeks of punishment, with sharks in the back of our minds. That's when the real test began.

Twelve-mile sand runs. Midnight surf torture. Getting hammered by boats and head-high waves crashing on top of you. You're not trying to win; you're trying to survive. I'll never forget Ely, a teammate who limped across the finish line Friday afternoon, casually complaining about a sore back. Turned out he'd fractured a vertebra on Wednesday and just kept going.

That's Hell Week. And here's the bridge to parenting: Raising kids isn't a sprint to age eighteen. It's a series of cold, dark swims, moments when they'll get lost in the black and look for a light—any light—to guide them back. Our job is to be that light. Steady. Unwavering. A quiet presence on the horizon that says, "Home is this way." You don't yell. You don't panic. You just keep swimming beside them, silent and strong, until they find their rhythm again. And then, if we've done our job well, they swim ahead.

On their own.

You've made it this far in the book, and that says something rare about you: commitment. You've seen the map, including my missteps, our family systems, the small wins stacked into bigger ones. Every lesson in these pages—discipline, purpose, resilience, environment, competence, digital defense—was shared to help you handle the hardest mission out there: raising humans who meet life with clarity, courage, and character.

But don't forget this lesson: Confidence is rarely born in comfort. It's forged in the moments when we leap into the unknown, the uncomfortable, the untested. Like that cold, dirty ice puddle Tyler jumped into one winter day in Tahoe. No hesitation, no overthinking. Just a splash, a shriek, and a smile. That's what this whole parenting thing is all about.

We're not here to raise kids who play it safe. We're here to raise puddle jumpers—the kind of humans who look at the world, see the risk, and leap anyway. Who get wet, get bruised, get back up, and say, "Let's go again."

Keep swimming. Keep showing up. Keep laughing when it's hard and listening when it matters. Your kids don't need a perfect captain. They need one who stays in the fight. Who keeps the guide light on. Who jumps first, so they know they can too.

This book is for the parents still out there in the storm, doing their best without applause. For the ones who patch scraped knees and broken hearts and keep going. For the stoic mom or dad who knows that the only thing harder than raising great kids is being there for them consistently, with love.

Thanks for swimming with me.

Now go raise some puddle jumpers.

Acknowledgments

This book is for the ones doing their best in a world that rarely gives gold stars for parenting: for those who lose sleep over decisions no one else sees. Who cry in the car sometimes but still walk in the door with a smile. Who set the alarm early to make pancakes or drive to a soccer game across town. Who discipline with love, fail with grace, and get back up because the mission doesn't stop when it gets messy—it starts.

You are the anchor. The quiet hero. The one who shows up.

And in case no one's told you lately, you're doing better than you think.

I want to give a huge thank you to my parents, Jack and Lynn. You did your best to raise a wild kid with big dreams and a habit of looking for trouble like a heat-seeking missile, and for that, I'm forever grateful. You gave me the grit and spine I needed to go out and face the world—thank you.

I'll never forget my mom teaching me to drive stick on the hills of Ventura. No coddling, no shortcuts, just her voice saying, "Come on, figure it out." I can still feel the panic of trying to balance brake, clutch, and gas with two feet on an incline so steep it felt like the car would roll backward forever. She stood firm—tough but kind, always supportive—forcing me to wrestle that clutch until I got it right. That lesson was about more than driving; it was about keeping calm under pressure, about learning the hard things because they'd matter later.

And my dad, those early wake-ups and dark Saturday drives to the hockey rink before the sun came up are burned into me. He was bone-tired from a week of hard work, but still showed up, thermos of coffee in hand. He never gave speeches about commitment or family—he lived it. That lesson stuck: Show up for your kids, even when it costs you. That's how you build a family that lasts.

To my three amazing kids, you're the reason behind every word in this book. You've taught me more about love, leadership, and patience than any SEAL mission ever could. And to Gretchen, my ex-wife and amazing co-parent, we may have gone our separate ways, but I'll always be grateful for the years of teamwork it took to raise such incredible humans. Thanks to your husband, Bobby, for being a rock-solid stepdad to our kids, too. Bob has always been present with discipline, heart, and consistency, and I respect the hell out of that.

To my YPO forum crew, Kent Collier, Kevin Tung, Jeremy Katz, Jeff Berger, Marco Achon, and Robert Roley, you've been more than mentors to my kids—you've been part of our village.

To my former writing partner, John Mann, still one of the most talented writers I've ever met, you pushed me to write harder, better, and with more guts. Being in your orbit made me sharper and gave me the confidence to set out on my own writing journey.

To my agent, David Moldawer, thank you for championing this project and reminding me that books only work if they bleed truth. You helped me hit that mark. And to Madeline, my badass publisher and co-founder at Author's Equity, thank you for believing I had something useful to say that wasn't just locker-room wisdom dressed in sniper camo.

Shout out to Don and Nina, the other founders of Author's Equity, for building something real and giving guys like me a place to tell stories that matter. And the rest of the AE crew: Rose (who wrangled deadlines like a lion tamer), Erin (the print whisperer), Andrea (voice of the audio realm), Carly, Sam, Sarah, and Maddy (who somehow did everything short of birthing this book herself). Craig and Deb, holding down sales and slinging this thing far and wide, you're all part of the puddle-jumper tribe now, like it or not.

A special thanks to my editor, Zach Gajewski, who not only brought sharp insight and structure to this book but also the perspective of a fellow parent with young kids of his own. Zach had the tough job of wrangling my stories and sorting through the madness to help me shape them into something clear and useful for parents everywhere. He did it with patience, precision, and a steady hand, and I couldn't have asked for a better partner in this process.

This book was a mission. And like any good op, it took a team of true pros to pull it off. I couldn't have done it without you. See you on the next jump.

Parenting Resources

The following pages are packed with reminders, field-tested resources, books, and movies that opened my kids' eyes to courage and character, and conversation starters that turn quiet car rides and long-distance phone calls into deep talks. Think of this section as the go-bag you keep by the door: quick to grab, loaded with essentials, ready whenever the next parenting challenge drops. Some of these tools will make you laugh, some will punch you in the gut, and all of them will help you keep the momentum we've built together throughout this book. Dive in, explore, and customize as you see fit.

Chapter Summaries and Guide

Eight Big Ideas, Said Simply

1. Cultivating Mental Strength

- Your words become their inner voice—keep a 5:1 ratio of positives to corrections.
- Praise effort ("You worked hard") over talent ("You're smart").
- Teach mental skills: visualization, mantras, and positive self-talk to replace negative loops and defend against outside noise.

Strong-Mind Formula:
Positive input + daily reps + reflection = strong mind

2. Building Confidence

- Let kids carry weight early: chores, swim, bike, pet care, small jobs.
- Mistakes teach more than success; talk through what they learned.
- Put them around good people, including mentors, coaches, and teammates.

Confidence Formula:
Failure + reflection + another rep = competence

3. Disciplining with Love

- Discipline and boundaries teach; punishment just penalizes.
- Explain the rule and the reason; use fair, natural consequences.
- Correct the behavior, protect the relationship, and stay united as parents.

Discipline Formula:
Clear limits + calm follow-through + connection = respect

4. Raising Kids with Purpose

- Don't hand them your map; help them draw their own and find their spark.
- Follow curiosity: Give them time, tools, and experiences.
- One trusted mentor can change a kid's path.

Spark Formula:
Curiosity + support + exploration = purpose

5. Modeling Healthy Habits

- Sleep is fuel; treat it like a performance tool.
- Real food first, water often; family meals connect everyone.
- Move daily: play, walk, stretch, sweat.

Healthy Habits Formula:
Sleep + real food + daily movement = strong body

6. Designing Digital Defense

- Model positive screen use and online safety—adults follow the same rules.
- Keep clear lines: device-free meals, no screens in bedrooms, early cutoff times.
- Teach digital street smarts: scams, predators, pornography, privacy.

Online-Safety Formula:
Clear rules + modeled behavior + open talk = digital safety

7. Talking About Sex, Drugs, and Alcohol

- Start real talks about the hard stuff early: sex, consent, drugs, alcohol, online risks.
- Ask open questions: "What's something you saw today that didn't feel right?"
- Have a "no-questions-asked" rule for rides home for safety.

Hard-Stuff Formula:
Early talks + honest tone + safe space = trust

8. Creating the Forever Family

- Family isn't a project with an end date; it's a lifelong team. Build a home your kids want to keep coming back to, not one they can't wait to leave.
- Shift from command to counsel as they grow: Guide more, control less, and let real-world lessons do the teaching.
- Teach responsibility early; money, work, and gratitude are learned best by doing, not lecturing.
- When they launch, stay their captain—steady, available, but not steering every move. Create a home base that feels like a magnet, not a museum.

Forever-Family Formula:
Love + consistency + shared experiences = lasting connection

Helpful Reminders and Tips

Instead of That, Say This

- "Be careful." → "What's your plan?"
- "Don't yell." → "Use a calm voice."
- "You're so smart." → "I saw how hard you worked."
- "You can't do this." → "You're learning—take the next step."

House Rules (Quick View)

- **Meals.** Device-free for everyone.
- **Bedrooms.** No personal screens overnight.
- **Daily.** Thirty minutes when the whole house is off devices.
- **Age Gates.** Phone around thirteen; social media in high school or later.
- **Safety.** Family code word and no-questions-asked ride home.
- **Online.** Teach about scams, pornography, predators; sometimes cowatch or coplay.

When a Problem Pops Up (Six Quick Steps)

1. Check yourself first. If you're emotionally heated, pause.
2. Check the kid's state. Can they listen now?
3. Hear the full story.
4. Pick the goal together ("What are we trying to fix?").
5. Choose a natural, fair consequence.
6. Repair by apologizing and move on by planning ahead for next time.

Weekly Habits That Work

- One new challenge without a rescue plan (age-safe risk).
- One consistent family ritual (dinner, walk, game) on the same day and time.
- One mentor touchpoint (call, visit, practice).
- One skill rep toward a goal.
- One "outside grit" moment: cold, rain, hills, or just a hard thing, experienced together.

PJ Pocket Reminders

- Prepare, don't protect.
- Consistency beats intensity.
- Environment beats willpower.
- Lead by example.
- Discipline builds freedom.

Puddle Jumper Principles

Fail Forward

Failure isn't the end; it's the tuition you pay for resilience. Every scraped knee, missed belt, or broken sink is practice for life. Tell your kids your own stories of stumbles and how you recovered so they know setbacks aren't stop signs—they are a necessary ingredient for success.

Ordinary Magic

The everyday stuff is where the real growth happens: sleepovers, backyard adventures, a trip to the store by themselves, swim lessons before they can walk. Don't wait for the big moments; the magic is in letting them jump into the messy puddles of life.

Jump In

Courage is built in the deep end. From asking for an autograph on the Portland airport carpet to skydiving out of a C-130 over the Yuma desert, kids learn confidence by doing. Let them take risks, get messy, and feel the rush of "I did it myself."

Build the Village

Your voice alone can fade into static. But a teacher, a coach, or even a neighbor with a killer tomato garden can change how your kid sees themselves. Don't go it alone—let mentors and community water the seeds you've planted.

Lead by Example

Kids don't follow instructions; they follow models. Show them grit, integrity, kindness, and hustle through your actions, whether that's apologizing after losing your cool in traffic or rolling out of bed at 5 a.m. to coach their team after a 60-hour workweek.

Let Them Own It

Responsibility sticks when kids feel the weight of their choices. Whether it's fixing what they broke or standing up to give a presentation they prepared themselves, step back enough for them to carry the load and discover their own strength.

Keep the Mic Open

Conversations beat lectures every time. The hard topics—sex, drugs, alcohol, digital chaos—require honesty, vulnerability, and a lot of listening. Keep the mic open so your kids know they can tell you anything without losing your love.

Let Them Write Their Own Story

Expose them to the world, then get out of the way. From debate halls to welding shops, gap years to college lecture halls, help your kids chase what lights them up. Purpose isn't a trophy, it's a torch—one they'll pass forward.

Health as a Foundation

You can't build resilience on junk food and four hours of sleep. Nutrition, rest, and movement aren't side notes; they're the engine. Teach them that what goes in their body powers what comes out in life.

Discipline with Empathy

Discipline teaches—punishment just penalizes. Like the monks of New Skete raising puppies with love and consistency, the goal is clarity, not fear. Correct in private, lead with love, and explain the "why" so the lesson lasts.

Confidence Is Earned

Confidence isn't gifted, it's built. Let them struggle, sweat, and succeed on their terms—the payoff is self-belief that sticks.

Own the Digital Feed

Screens aren't going anywhere, so help your kids own their feed instead of being owned by it. Teach them early that likes aren't love and algorithms aren't identity. Digital resilience is just as vital as physical.

How We Talk Matters

The soundtrack we play in our kids' heads becomes their inner voice for life. Every "I believe in you" or "You've got this" sticks deeper than we realize. Choose positive words that build courage and connection—they will echo for longer than you think.

Let Them Soar

At some point, you've got to let go. Give them the skills, then trust them to take flight—whether that's heading off to college, backpacking across Europe, or just biking to the corner store. Your job is to help them grow their wings, not clip them.

Goal-Setting Template

Vision Statement

Goals

School

1.
2.
3.

Personal

1.
2.
3.

Family

1.
2.
3.

Three-Year Goals

1.
2.
3.

Remember, goals should be specific and measurable ("Get above 90 percent on my next math test" versus "Get a better grade in math"). Start with just three in each category to make them simple and achievable without becoming overwhelming.

Navy SEAL Dad Tips to Keep Your Kids Safe

When it comes to your kids' safety, a little preparation goes a long way. Here are some items and resources I provided my kids with over the years to give them an edge in the real world:

- **High-Powered Flashlight.** Not your average keychain light, I'm talking 1000 lumens minimum, bright enough to blind someone in broad daylight. Compact, legal to carry anywhere, and an underrated self-defense tool. Surefire makes some of the best.
- **Bulletproof Backpack Insert.** Look for a US-made NIJ Level IIIA insert. When paired with a laptop or a stack of books, it can stop handgun rounds and even help slow down a rifle shot in worst-case scenarios. It's a grim reality, but one worth preparing for.
- **Defensive Driving School.** I taught my kids what I'd learned from attending offensive and defensive driver training, but I wish I had sent them to a legit one-week defensive race car driving school. Having them go through it would have been a great confidence booster and given them some incredible skills to make them much safer drivers.
- **Family Code Word.** This is especially important now that AI can replicate voices. If someone calls your kid claiming there's an emergency and it sounds like you, the code word is your first line of defense. (The same goes if someone calls you claiming to be your child.)
- **Martial Arts Training.** Martial arts provide self-defense, but they also build confidence, awareness, discipline, and resilience. Whether it's jujitsu, Muay Thai, or traditional karate, getting your kid on the mat gives them both skills and presence.

Recommended Books to Prepare Kids for Life (10+ Years)

Alaska by James Michener
Anything by Michener is incredible. He writes historically accurate fiction that's immersive and rich. Every history class should be teaching this book.

The Alchemist by Paulo Coelho
A young shepherd follows his personal legend across the desert. This book is poetic, deep, and perfect for kids ready to explore the idea of destiny and self-trust. Give it to them once they can handle some abstraction.

Atomic Habits: An Easy & Proven Way to Build Good Habits & Break Bad Ones by James Clear
A great book for kids to learn how powerful habits can be. Shows how small changes compound into big results.

The Boy Who Harnessed the Wind by William Kamkwamba
True story of a boy in Malawi who built a windmill to save his village. Inspires creativity, resilience, and self-belief.

Daring Greatly: How the Courage to Be Vulnerable Transforms the Way We Live, Love, Parent, and Lead by Brené Brown
This one is teen friendly with guidance, as it requires a little maturity, but it's gold. Helps kids understand that vulnerability isn't weakness; it's the doorway to courage, connection, and growth.

Do Hard Things: A Teenage Rebellion Against Low Expectations by Alex and Brett Harris

Written by two teenage brothers, this book challenges teens to step up, ditch low expectations, and pursue something bigger than comfort.

Drive: The Surprising Truth About What Motivates Us by Daniel Pink

Breaks down what actually motivates people (spoiler: it's not rewards and punishments). A must read for teens and the parents trying to understand them.

Eleven Rings: The Soul of Success by Phil Jackson

Great book on leadership. Here's what my son Jackson had to say about it: "Great to read about Kobe, Shaq, and Jordan, but it was amazing to see what goes on behind the scenes to cultivate greatness."

Endurance: Shackleton's Incredible Voyage by Alfred Lansing

One of the greatest true survival stories ever told. Shows what leadership, perseverance, and trust in your team look like when things fall apart. Great for teens who think quitting is the easiest option.

Getting Things Done: The Art of Stress-Free Productivity by David Allen

My son Jackson said this book was transformational for starting high school. Allen provides a tactical system that helps kids organize their mental clutter and take control of their time before it controls them.

The Giver by Lois Lowry

A modern classic. Challenges kids to think critically about freedom, conformity, and the price of comfort. It's fiction with real weight, and the book always sparks deep conversation.

Grit: The Power of Passion and Perseverance by Angela Duckworth
Based on research from high performers across every field, this is an excellent book to teach kids that consistent effort matters more than raw talent.

Hatchet by Gary Paulsen
A survival story that kicks off with a plane crash, forcing a kid to learn how to fend for himself. Teaches problem-solving, grit, and the power of adapting fast. Also shows the shift from panic to presence.

How to Win Friends and Influence People by Dale Carnegie
An incredible book for young adults to read, especially before they start ninth grade. Helps build social confidence and emotional intelligence.

Jonathan Livingston Seagull by Richard Bach
A short, fictional story about a seagull who refuses to live an average life. Teaches courage, nonconformity, and the pursuit of purpose. One of those "read it when they're young, reread it when they're older" type of books.

The Making of a Navy SEAL: My Story of Surviving the Toughest Challenge and Training the Best (Youth Edition) by Brandon Webb
This is the young reader edition of my bestselling memoir, *The Red Circle: My Life in the Navy SEAL Sniper Corps and How I Trained America's Deadliest Marksmen*. Scholastic has it in their library. Great for teaching grit, leadership, and real-world resilience.

The Mamba Mentality: How I Play by Kobe Bryant
This book is about more than basketball; it's about legacy, obsession, precision, and finding your edge. Great for athletes or any kid who's wired for performance and wants to understand what elite commitment looks like.

Man's Search for Meaning by Viktor Frankl
For older teens. A Holocaust survivor and psychiatrist, Frankl explains how purpose can pull you through the darkest moments in life. Heavy but life-changing.

Mastering Fear: A Navy SEAL's Guide by Brandon Webb and John David Mann
I wrote this book after teaching my best friend, Kamal, how to swim in his forties. He told me, "Dude, you changed my life; you have to write about this." It covers the basics of mental management and reframes fear as a necessary component to success.

Memory Book: The Classic Guide to Improving Your Memory at Work, at School, and at Play by Harry Lorayne
We taught this book as a class in Navy SEAL sniper school, and I gave it to all my kids. It's super practical for everyday life, and in schoolwork, it's a secret weapon.

Mindset: The New Psychology of Success by Carol Dweck
The book that coined the term "growth mindset." Helps kids (and adults) understand that abilities are built, not fixed. The sooner they get this concept, the more risks they'll take and the better they'll rebound from setbacks.

The Obstacle Is the Way: The Timeless Art of Turning Trials into Triumph by Ryan Holiday
Ryan is a great guy, and I've been on his podcast before. What I love about this book for kids is that it shows them the value of overcoming obstacles in life—and that it's all part of growing up.

The Outsiders by S. E. Hinton
Still relevant decades after it was written. Shows kids what it means to form real bonds, question systems, and find loyalty in unexpected places. Fiction, but full of life lessons.

Peak: Secrets from the New Science of Expertise by Anders Ericsson and Robert Pool
The science behind elite performance. This book shows that greatness isn't born, it's trained through deliberate practice. Helps kids realize talent is just a starting point.

Range: Why Generalists Triumph in a Specialized World by David Epstein
For kids who haven't "found their thing" yet. Makes the case for trying many things before specializing; ideal for parents who are worried their kids are unfocused.

Refuse to Quit: A Female Navy SEALs Story by Brandon Webb
I wrote this novel about the first group of women to go through SEAL training. I wanted it to be an inspirational book for young women, and I had my own daughter, Madison, in mind when I wrote it.

Rich Dad, Poor Dad: What the Rich Teach Their Kids About Money—That the Poor and Middle Class Do Not! by Robert Kiyosaki
Teaches kids about personal finance and investing—the earlier they understand money, the better.

The 7 Habits of Highly Effective Teens by Sean Covey
A field manual for self-leadership. Breaks down core habits like prioritizing, goal-setting, and staying accountable—perfect for middle and high schoolers.

Shoe Dog: A Memoir by the Creator of Nike by Phil Knight

I love this book because it's a brand every kid knows, and Knight teaches perseverance and belief in your own vision, even when no one else sees it yet.

Stolen Focus: Why You Can't Pay Attention—and How to Think Deeply Again by Johann Hari

Essential reading for understanding how phones, apps, and tech hijack attention. Gives teens (and parents) tools to reclaim their mental clarity.

Tools of Titans: The Tactics, Routines, and Habits of Billionaires, Icons, and World-Class Performers by Tim Ferriss

I gave this book to all my kids after I finished reading it myself because it's such a great reference book with so many different personalities; it's sure to appeal, in part, to all kids' interests.

What Do You Do with a Problem? by Kobi Yamada

For younger kids, an illustrated story about courage and problem-solving. Helps reframe fear and anxiety into opportunity.

With Winning in Mind by Lanny Bassham

One of my favorites on mental mastery and an easy read. Teaches how to train your mindset like a champion.

The War of Art: Break Through the Blocks and Win Your Inner Creative Battles by Steven Pressfield

Perfect for older teens, this book breaks down what stops us from doing the work we're meant to do and how to fight back. It's about resistance, purpose, and the discipline to sit down and build something that matters.

Parenting Reading Pro Tips

Having trouble getting your kids to read? Sometimes we have to properly motivate them with irresistible incentives. New phone upgrade? Read three books and write a report on each. Want that new gadget or a trip with your friends to the water park or wind tunnel? You get the idea. Every time my kids would come to me with a request, I'd trade it for a book or two; eventually, they knew this was the cost of doing business with Dad. And to this day, they still remember the books I recommended to them and the impact they had on their lives.

Audiobooks also work great for active kids, especially those with ADHD (like my son Tyler). Consider gifting them a MasterClass subscription around age ten. Let your kids explore what lights them up: film, business, writing, design. It's a modern way to expose them to world-class mentorship.

Movies and TV Shows to Watch Together

Toddlerhood (2–4 Years)

Bluey (series)—Short, smart, and wildly underrated. It shows parents and kids how to play, solve problems, and be emotionally aware without the usual sugar-coated fluff.

Curious George—Chaos with purpose. Shows kids how to explore, ask questions, and learn through experience.

Daniel Tiger's Neighborhood—Teaches little kids how to name their feelings and handle frustration like tiny emotional ninjas.

Finding Nemo—Teaches courage, independence, and what it means to keep going, even when everything feels overwhelming.

The Gruffalo—Smart storytelling that shows kids how to outthink fear instead of just running from it.

The Many Adventures of Winnie the Pooh—Teaches emotional safety, patience, and friendship, without trying too hard.

Moana—A kid who doesn't wait for permission to find out who she is. Big message: The world doesn't define you—you do.

Puffin Rock—Calm, nature focused, and perfect for slowing things down while still learning about the real world.

Sesame Street—Still elite. Teaches everything from empathy to counting to how to live in a diverse world.

Zog—A clumsy dragon learns that effort beats perfection. Great for early lessons on grit and resilience.

Early Childhood (4–6 Years)

Brave—Strong female lead. Real consequences. Lessons about humility, owning your mistakes, and family.

Charlotte's Web—Death, loyalty, and deep friendship in a way kids can actually process. A heavy story done right.

Frozen—Yeah, it's everywhere. But it nails the tension between freedom and fear, and how love doesn't always look like a fairy tale.

How to Train Your Dragon—Teaches empathy and courage, especially when it means standing up against your own tribe.

Inside Out—Teaches kids that all emotions matter, not just the happy ones. If you want emotionally intelligent humans, start here.

The Iron Giant—One of the best movies ever at teaching identity, sacrifice, and choosing who you want to be.

The Lorax—Shows kids how to speak up, protect what matters, and think about the planet they're growing up on.

The Lego Movie—Wild creativity, teamwork, and a takedown of rigid thinking. (Also, just a blast to watch.)

My Neighbor Totoro—A weirdly beautiful way to talk about grief, wonder, and the healing power of imagination.

Paddington—Teaches decency without preaching. Paddington is the role model we all secretly need.

Middle Childhood (6–10 Years)

Akeelah and the Bee—A great story about confidence, hard work, and owning your voice in the face of pressure.

Coco—Purpose, legacy, and honoring your roots. Kids need to understand where they come from to know where they're going.

The Karate Kid—The original growth-mindset movie. Shows what consistent effort, humility, and a great mentor can do.

Kung Fu Panda—Funny but powerful. Shows how believing in yourself changes everything, even when you don't look the part.

Matilda—Intelligence, standing up to abuse, and using your brain to fight back.

The Sandlot—Classic boyhood story. Friendship, facing fear, and summer freedom.

Spider-Man: Into the Spider-Verse—Identity, responsibility, and the idea that anyone can rise to the occasion.

WALL-E—Environmental responsibility and emotional connection with almost no dialogue. Visually brilliant and surprisingly deep.

Wonder—Teaches kids to lead with kindness and look beyond the surface. It should be mandatory viewing in schools.

Zootopia—Smashes stereotypes and shows that real courage means asking hard questions.

Preadolescence (10–12 Years)

Apollo 13—Real-life problem-solving under pressure. Great for showing how critical thinking saves lives.

Bridge to Terabithia—Beautiful and heartbreaking. Helps kids process loss, friendship, and imagination.

Hidden Figures—Teaches brains, courage, and speaking truth to power. Especially important for girls.

Life of Pi—Survival, spirituality, and storytelling—deep, but totally worth watching with a curious kid.

The Martian—Science meets survival. Shows how calm under pressure and persistence win the day.

October Sky—A kid who goes from coal miner to rocket scientist. Great for showing how dreams plus effort beat the odds.

The Pursuit of Happyness—A brutal, honest look at perseverance and fatherhood. Shows what it means to fight for a better life.

Secondhand Lions—A weirdly perfect movie about honor, risk-taking, and living a life of purpose.

The Secret Life of Walter Mitty—Teaches courage, imagination, and breaking out of comfort zones.

To Kill a Mockingbird—Still hits hard. Teaches moral courage and standing up for what's right, even when it costs you.

Adolescence (12–18 Years)

Boyhood—A slow burn that mirrors how life actually unfolds: messy, beautiful, and complicated.

Dead Poets Society—Purpose, voice, and learning to think for yourself. I wish every teen watched this before high school graduation.

Good Will Hunting—Emotional wounds, raw talent, and the power of real mentorship. "It's not your fault" still gets me.

The Hate U Give—Heavy, important, and real. Talks about justice, activism, and finding your voice.

The Perks of Being a Wallflower—Mental health, identity, and learning to live with your whole story.

Remember the Titans—Leadership, unity, and fighting for something bigger than yourself. Still one of the best.

The Social Network—Ambition without accountability. Shows what happens when ego outpaces empathy.

Stand by Me—Friendship, trauma, and that liminal space between childhood and whatever comes next.

The Way Way Back—Coming-of-age under pressure. Proves how one adult believing in you can change everything.

Whiplash—A look at what excellence really costs, and the fine line between greatness and obsession.

Conversation Starters

Toddlerhood (2–4 Years)

Focus: Independence and Emotional Control

1. "How did that make you feel? Can you show me your face?" Gives them a concrete way to name emotions before they have a big vocabulary.
2. "Can you help me with this job? I can't do it without you." Sparks autonomy and responsibility in bite-sized form.
3. "What color is your feeling right now?" Turns abstract emotions into visuals toddlers understand.
4. "Can you tell me what made you smile today?" Trains early gratitude and positive recall.
5. "Do you want to try again or ask for help?" Teaches the fail-recover loop instead of meltdown-quit.
6. "What can we do when we feel mad instead of yelling?" Rehearses healthy coping before the next eruption.
7. "What sound does your happy/sad/mad feeling make?" Adds a playful sensory layer to emotion ID.
8. "Can you tell me about your favorite thing you did today?" Builds narrative skills and self-reflection.
9. "Where do your big feelings go when you're done with them?" Begins the concept of letting emotions pass.
10. "Can you show me how you calm yourself?" Introduces self-soothing as a superpower, not a punishment.

Early Childhood (4–6 Years)

Focus: Social Skills and Empathy

1. "What's something nice you did for a friend today?" Reinforces kindness as a daily practice.
2. "If someone is being left out at school, what would you do?" Rehearses social courage before it's needed.
3. "How would you feel if someone did that to you?" Encourages classic role-reversal to wire empathy.
4. "Can you think of a time you helped someone feel better?" Links action to emotional impact.
5. "What's the best part of being a friend?" Gets them defining friendship values early.
6. "How can we make someone smile today?" Turns empathy into a mini mission.
7. "What's something you can do to make a new friend?" Moves from passive hope to proactive connection.
8. "If your toys had feelings, what would they say?" Creates a safe sandbox for discussing emotions indirectly.
9. "What's a way you helped someone without being asked?" Encourages initiative and a service mindset.
10. "How do you show someone you care about them?" Bridges thought and action in relationships.

Middle Childhood (6–10 Years)

Focus: Responsibility and Problem-Solving

1. "What's one thing that was hard today, and how did you handle it?" Normalizes struggle as data, not drama.
2. "If you were in charge of the house for a day, what would the rules be?" Lets them test leadership in theory first.
3. "What's something new you learned this week?" Keeps growth mindset on the radar.

4. "What do you do when you make a mistake?" Shifts the spotlight to recovery plans, not blame.
5. "Can you think of a time you solved a problem all by yourself?" Banks confidence for future challenges.
6. "What's something you're proud of, big or small?" Trains intrinsic reward over external praise.
7. "What's one rule you think is really important, and why?" Builds ethical reasoning, not blind obedience.
8. "What's something you tried even though it was hard?" Celebrates effort over outcome—core grit currency.
9. "How do you know when to ask for help?" Teaches tactical humility, not helplessness.
10. "What would you teach someone your age about being responsible?" Peer-teaching cements their own standards.

Preadolescence (10–12 Years)

Focus: Self-Identity and Peer Relationships

1. "When did you last stand up for something that felt right?" Surfaces value-driven action stories.
2. "What kind of friend do you want to be, and why?" Moves them from having friends to being one.
3. "What's something you wish adults understood about kids?" Opens a feedback loop and shows respect.
4. "How do you handle it when your friends make bad choices?" Rehearses boundary setting before peer pressure spikes.
5. "What are the three most important values to you?" Starts building an internal compass.
6. "What's something about yourself you're still figuring out?" Normalizes identity exploration.
7. "What's something you've changed your mind about recently?" Encourages intellectual flexibility over stubbornness.

8. "Who makes you feel like you can be your real self, and why?" Identifies safe allies and models authenticity.
9. "What's one thing you've done that took real courage?" Catalogs bravery, creating evidence for future self-talk.
10. "If you could give advice to a younger kid, what would you tell them?" Turns reflection into mentorship.

Adolescence (12–18 Years)

Focus: Decision-Making and Future Planning

1. "What's a mistake you made recently, and what did it teach you?" Shifts "failure" into strategic intel.
2. "If nothing could stop you, what would you go after, and what's in your way?" Maps ambition plus limiting beliefs.
3. "What kind of life do you want to build, and why?" Zooms out to long-term vision.
4. "When do you feel the most confident?" Locates peak-state environments they can replicate.
5. "What scares you about the future, and how can you prepare?" Couples vulnerability with action planning.
6. "How do you define success for yourself?" Encourages personal metrics over borrowed ones.
7. "What does freedom mean to you right now?" Explores autonomy with accountability.
8. "How do you want to be remembered by people your age?" Introduces legacy thinking in real time.
9. "What's a choice you made that helped you grow?" Reinforces deliberate, growth-oriented risk.
10. "If your life were a movie right now, what would the title be?" Provides fun framing that reveals self-narrative.

Parents with Adult Kids

Focus: Mutual Respect and Lifelong Connection

1. "What's something you've learned recently that surprised you, even about yourself?" Keeps the relationship rooted in growth, not nostalgia.
2. "Is there anything I did as a parent that helped you or held you back?" Invites an honest audit and possible healing.
3. "What kind of support do you need from me these days, if any?" Acknowledges their autonomy while staying available as a parent.
4. "What's a risk you've been thinking about taking, and what's holding you back?" Positions you as a sounding board, not a backseat driver.
5. "What's something about your childhood you look back on differently now?" Explores evolving perspectives without defensiveness.
6. "How do you define success for yourself right now?" Aligns expectations with their current values, not yours.
7. "What's one thing I could do better to support our relationship as adults?" Models lifelong growth and humility.
8. "If you became a parent tomorrow, what's one thing you'd do the same, or different, from how I raised you?" Sparks generational learning—and humor.
9. "What are you most proud of in your life right now?" Gives them the center stage and recognition.
10. "Is there anything you've ever wanted to ask me, but never did?" Opens the vault for deeper trust and closure.

Money Tools for Kids

If you want to teach money the puddle jumpers way, it has to be real. No lecture—actual reps with actual responsibility. That's where these tools come in. These tools provide a simple way to practice earning, spending, saving, and screwing up a little while the stakes are still small. Think of these as training wheels for financial independence. You're still the coach, but now they've got a bike to ride.

Acorns Early

Acorns Early is built for kids roughly six to eighteen and gives them a debit card plus a simple system for chores and allowance. Parents set the guardrails; kids do the earning and spending. It fits the "confidence is earned" philosophy because they learn by doing, not by being rescued.

Greenlight

Greenlight is another strong option for allowance, chores, and spending controls. It lets parents tie money to tasks and track what kids do with it, while still giving the kid ownership.

BusyKid

BusyKid combines chores, allowance automation, and a kid card, with a nice emphasis on learning to split money into spending, saving, giving, and even investing.

About the Author

Brandon Webb is a father of three happy humans and a tactical toy poodle named Apollo. He's also a combat-decorated Navy SEAL sniper, a multiple *New York Times* bestselling author, and a Harvard Business School alumnus.

Keep Building Strong Kids

This book is a starting line, not the finish. If you want to keep raising capable, confident kids and build a stronger family, the work continues beyond these pages.

Continue here:
puddlejumpersparenting.com.

There you'll find

- **My free newsletter, *The Puddle Jumper Brief***, with weekly lessons, practical tools, and real-world stories
- **The Puddle Jumpers course and community**, for deeper training and support